What Others Are Saying

Mother, minister, teacher, and author Roz Brown writes *So You Wanna Be a Help Meet? Act Like a Godly Woman and Think Like Christ*. Brown's book is an honest look at preparing for marriage, waiting on God's timing for His best, and drawing near to Christ throughout the process.

With a combination of scriptures and real-life experiences, readers are provoked to search their own hearts regarding their motives for marriage and encouraged to draw near to Christ and model their lives after Him.

The book encourages readers to be honest with God, take a look at their relational history, and commit their future and heart's desire for marriage to the Lord. This is a must-read for any woman considering, desiring, or even just wanting to know more about marriage!

—Julie Karanja
Missouri
The Light House Outreach Coordinator and Counselor

Roz Brown really did a fantastic job writing a book that is easy and enjoyable to read, but most importantly, she has stayed faithful and true to the principles in God's Word. This book is practical and helpful for everyone seeking God's best regarding their future. I was impressed with her boldness and courage to apply God's timeless truths in ever-changing times.

It is not popular or easy to do things God's way, but I am confident that if the readers will follow the advice given in this book, they will reap a bountiful harvest of peace and blessings in their personal lives. You will be richly blessed when you read this book!

On a side note, I would also like to say that Roz lives these principles in her own life and is a good example to every life she touches. Roz hasn't just written a book—she has lived it.

—Cindy Brooks
Women's Ministry
Southview Baptist Church

Rosiland has poured numerous pearls of wisdom into this book. If you are contemplating marriage, this is a must-read, especially chapter 6! You will be blessed! I like the questions and pages for journaling! Awesome book!

—Ruffina Rector, RN

SO YOU WANNA BE
A HELP MEET?

SO YOU WANNA BE A HELP MEET?

ACT LIKE A GODLY WOMAN AND THINK LIKE CHRIST

ROZ BROWN

So You Wanna Be a Help Meet?
Copyright © 2017 by Roz Brown.
Republished by Imperium Publishing © 2018.

All rights reserved. No part of this publication may be reproduced, distributed, or transmitted in any form or by any means, including photocopying, recording, or other electronic or mechanical methods, without the prior written permission of the copyright holder, except in the case of brief quotations embodied in critical reviews and certain other noncommercial uses permitted by copyright law. For permission requests, write to the publisher, addressed "Attention: Permissions Coordinator," at the address below.

All Scripture quotations, unless otherwise indicated, are taken from the *Holy Bible, King James Version,* Cambridge, 1769. Used by permission. All rights reserved.

ISBN: 978-1-64318-007-6

Imperium Publishing
1097 N. 400th Rd
Baldwin City, KS, 66006

www.imperiumpublishing.com

Dedication

This book is dedicated to two very important people in my life: my daughter, Travina L. Jarvis (Tricy) and my son, David J. Mitchell (DJ).

Travina, from the very moment that I knew I was pregnant, I have loved you. My life would not be the same without you. You are everything I have ever wanted to be and much more. You are a fearless, strong, confident, beautiful, educated, and committed Christian woman. I am so very proud of the woman and mother you've become. To my bold "eager to take the world by its tail," outstanding daughter, I dedicate this book to you, my love, my sweet pea.

Love, Mama

DJ, what can I say? You have certainly surpassed my expectations of you as a young man. DJ, I love you so very much. I am so very proud of you. Watching God work through your life is amazing to me. You are educated, talented, creative, and witty. You have always had my heart in your hands. To the boy who wanted to be He-Man, Batman, Spiderman, and Superman with a homemade cape, there you would go running through the house, carrying my heart in your hands, and there you've had it all your life. This book I dedicate to you also, my son and my heart.

Love, Mama

Acknowledgment

To Dawn N. Patterson, JD for your unfailing and undying support on this project. Assisting me in editing this book was no easy task; when reading my unedited nonmarginal script was difficult, you saw the beauty and importance of this book. Thank you for believing in me when I had doubts.

Thank you for assisting me in completing the vision that I believed God gave me and for helping me write the words in a way when I wasn't always sure how to say them.

Thank you very much for your support, love, and prayers.

—Mama Roz

Contents

Foreword 13
Preface 15
Introduction 19

1   What is Your Why? 21
2   Behavior Befitting a Godly Woman 36
3   Why Wait on God? 48
4   Who Is Your All in All, Your Everything? 60
5   Prepare Ye the Way! 69
6   Bye-Bye Baggage! 79
7   Closing Statement 105
8   Holiday Heartburn 116
9   On Lockdown 128
10 Red Flags Mean Stop! 140
11 Choose Me! 160
12 Expectations 168
13 Fireproof Your Relationship (Ephesians 6:10–17) 186
14 Dream Big! 193
15 Now That You Know 199

Afterword 201
About the Author 203

Foreword

In a fallen world, the truth is not popular. It is because of that fact that books like the one you hold in your hand are becoming harder to find. Let this foreword serve as a warning to all who would look for their corrupt skin to be scratched and their worldly views validated. If you're looking for the same old feminized female-empowerment drivel, you won't find it here.

Instead, Roz Brown brings the rare and so refreshing truth about God's perfect plan for His most beautiful creation. Roz exposes the amazing beauty and influence that awaits those ladies with the courage to obey God and shame the devil.

As her pastor, I have watched Roz hold herself to the same timeless standards that fill this book. It is with great conviction and awe that she performs her calling as an author. Only writing what she knows to be grounded in the Word of truth, Roz has a passion to see single women obtain the victory in Jesus that comes only in obedience to Him.

If you're tired of being churched by the usual suspects that seem to be consumed with their own success and glory,

I highly recommend this book as a no-nonsense road map to the greatest achievement a wife can obtain in the eyes of Almighty God.

—Michael Sean Brooks
Senior Pastor, Southview Baptist Church

Preface

This book *So You Wanna Be a Help Meet? Act Like a Godly Woman and Think Like Christ!* is written to women of all walks of life, religions, and ethnic backgrounds who desire to be married to men! (Yes, I said *men* because I know that marriage was ordained by God to be between a man and a woman. He said it in Genesis 2:18, 20–25, and again he reiterates marriage is between a man and women in Mark 10:6–9.)

Dating, engagement, wedding, marriage, and love are all words that excite women. Many times, even the desire alone to hear those words will cause women to compromise who they are and what they believe just to be a bride. I would like to share something with you as it relates to women's and men's thinking regarding starting a life together. The woman is excited about the wedding, the man is excited about the honeymoon, and both of them are clueless about the marriage, and the marriage is what you live! Have you ever heard of wedding counseling or honeymoon counseling? No, you haven't, and neither have I. Have you heard of premarital counseling? Well, that is what it is called. It is the process of receiving counseling as soon-to-be husband and wife before you get married.

This book is written for the same purpose that premarital counseling is recommended. It is to educate, encourage, and inspire you to seek and include God in your relationship from the first time your eyes meet his all the way to the wedding altar, if God chooses that plan for your life. It is my utmost prayer that the words within this book will change your thinking, thereby changing your life. If you desire to be married, chances are the desire will still be there after you finish reading this book. You simply will not be willing to settle for the first guy that asks you to marry him and you'll be honest enough to ask yourself the difficult question "are you even ready to be a wife?" but not just a wife, a godly wife. There truly is a difference. Being a wife according to the Word of God is more than just getting married, having sex, having children, and taking care of the family home. It is a lifetime commitment to serve God in a capacity that is very fulfilling and yet overwhelming at the same time.

In this book, you will learn what God's expectations are of you as a godly woman desiring to be married. You will learn what it takes to support your husband in marriage. Wives are considered the *help meet* because God requires them to help support their husbands in all areas of his life so that he can become the man, husband, and father that God has created him to be. I speak candidly and from the heart as God gives me deeper revelations of this matter through His Word, the Bible.

Invest in yourself as a woman and your future family by studying this book, praying while reading it along with your Bible, and seeking God with your whole heart regarding marriage and the physical, mental, emotional, and spiritual preparations for it. It is truly a life worth living if God is in the center of your relationship. "A threefold cord is not quickly broken" (Ecclesiastes 4:12).

By the end of our journey together, I pray that you will think of dating, your engagement, your wedding, your marriage, love, and your husband-to-be just as Christ does. "Let this mind be in you which was also in Christ Jesus" (Philippians 2:5).

Introduction

And ye shall know the truth,
and the truth shall make you free.

—John 8:32

"It is not good that the man should be alone; I will make [a] help meet for him" (Genesis 2:18). According to *Strong's Concordance, help meet* means "a helper suitable for him."

When I began writing this book several years ago, it was because I had read several books on love, marriage and dating, None of these books seem to really talk about what God had to say about the issues of love, marriage and dating. Many of these books had no biblical foundation and gave advice that violated God's Word.

Shortly after reading a few of these books, I remember having a conversation with one of my spiritual daughters about this subject. I became frustrated because women were being led astray. In the midst of my frustration, she challenged me to do something about it. I knew that the only way to combat untruth was with truth; not my truth; but God's truth. I knew then that a book that reveals God's expectations about how you should walk and talk in regard to your relationship with Christ and those around you was essential.

After reading this book, my prayer is that you will know that God loves you and wants you to have the very best in life. My prayer is that this book will set you free to make right decisions based on God's truth, which is the only truth that matters. Yes, God created us to have free will in the daily choices we make. My prayer is that after reading this book, you will choose God's way every day.

1

WHAT IS YOUR WHY?

*Call unto me and I will answer thee and shew thee
great and mighty things which thou knowest not.*

—Jeremiah 33:33

If you are reading this book, it is because you desire to be married; either you're dating, engaged or just dreaming of marriage. I am sure you have read a lot of books on marriage, ways to get a man's attention, how to keep a man's attention, and how to get him to marry you. There is no doubt in my mind that if you are reading *this* book, those books did not provide all the answers you were looking for. If they did, you would have no need to purchase another book on the subject! You may have also purchased this book because you thought those other books had all the answers you thought you needed. So you got married, but then the marriage did not work. Then again, you may be reading this book because you've yet to receive a proposal of marriage, and you don't know why. Well, whatever the reason for your having this book (even if it is a gift), you have to know that you have it because God needs you to read it in this season of your life.

God is waiting to take you on a wonderful journey of discovery. I am simply your tour guide. We will explore His truth through study, prayer, meditation, and maybe even some tears and laughter as we learn what we should be looking for in a godly man and what a godly man should be looking for in us. We will soon understand and know God's expectations of us while we wait. What we do with those expectations will determine whether we receive God's best for our lives now and throughout the years to come.

Are you scared yet? You should be. No, I'm just kidding, but you should take every word in this book seriously and be excited about learning what God does and does not want for you while you wait for God to bring you the man that He desires for you to marry.

I have a quiz for you. In the space below, answer the questions listed. In writing your answer, you must exclude the word *sex* as a reason for wanting to get married. You must also exclude the word *submit* from your answer on why you do not want to get married. Oh yeah, God already knows your reasons. He just wants to see if you will be honest with yourself and Him. Ready? Set? Write!

1. So why do I want to get married?

___

___

___

___

___

___

___

2. Why do I want to stay single?

___

___

___

___

___

___

___

Review your answers before moving on and make sure your answers reflect how you truly feel. Again, answer honestly, remembering that marriage is a big responsibility and a lifelong commitment if you plan on living by God's expectations and His Word. For the record, if you cannot be honest with yourself and God in answering those two questions, then there's a good chance you will not be honest with the man you love about the matter either.

What was the purpose of this quiz? Every woman has a reason for why she desires to be married. What's yours? The first purpose of this book is to help you determine why you want to get married in the first place, especially if this is not your first marriage. Answering the question "Why?" is crucial in any decision you make in life. When you know your *why* in any situation, you have truth, and truth will make you free (John 8:32) if you embrace it. Therefore, knowing why you want to get married will help you base your decision on truth. People get married for many reasons. Has it ever occurred to you that the reasons men get married are oftentimes very different from women's? Now that is something to think about.

If you are engaged (i.e., he actually proposed marriage to you, and you said yes), ask your fiancé (1) why he wants to get married, (2) why he wants to marry you, and (3) why did he propose now. When you ask him, just be prepared to answer question numbers 1 and 2. For question number 3, he may want to know why you accepted his proposal now. Even if he does not ask you those questions, see if his reasons are the same as yours.

I am sure his answer to question number 1 is because he loves you. That is a good answer, but it is not a good enough answer. Is one of the reasons for getting married stated that this is God's plan for your life? That must be the number one reason people get married. You can both love each other and still be out of God's will, simply because marriage is not in God's plan for either or both of you at this particular time in your lives. On the other hand, marriage may be in God's immediate plans for both of you but just not to each other, meaning God has chosen other spouses for you two to marry. Please be prepared to follow God's lead no matter what God asks of you.

Honestly answering the question, "Why do I want to get married?" will prompt you to answer the next question, "Should I get married?" We rush into marriage before we truly understand the expectations and requirements of marriage. We see people all around us getting married, and what we are really excited about is the wedding day: the gown, the colors, the flowers, the reception, the food, the music, the gifts, the bridal showers, and everyone's attention on the bride. Let's be honest. There is nothing like a beautiful wedding. The excitement can be overwhelming at times. I should know. I was a wedding coordinator for many years, and it was exciting for me, from helping the bride pick out her wedding gown to choosing the colors. It just does not get any better than planning and participating in a wedding. Oh, let's not forget the engagement ring! It all starts with the engagement ring so we think. The journey to the altar actually starts with God telling both of you that this is His plan for both of you at this time in your lives. You will probably need a minute to meditate on that, especially if you have not yet consulted with God on the matter.

So I will ask the question again. Why do you really want to get married? You do not have to answer now. You will have many opportunities to think and pray about your why throughout this book. The reasons for getting married cannot be based upon reasons and explanations given by your mom, dad, best friend, or even your pastor. You must get your answers from God and God alone, for God knows the *who, what, where, when, how, why* regarding your season of marriage and your life, period. He knows your real why, and He will help you understand if your reasons are within or outside of His will for your life at this time.

Yes, I know that the scripture is clear in that if you cannot contain yourself (e.g., from sex), you should marry (1 Corinthians 7:9). That's fine, but is sex the only thing you want to have in common in a lifelong relationship? I ask this question because there may come a time in your life when sex is not an available option for reasons beyond your or his control. Then what?

You will not know if this wonderful institution created by God is your true destiny until you can truthfully answer why you want to live a life that has to be completely selfless for the rest of your life. You may be asking, "Why is marriage a 'life that has to be completely selfless'?" Well, in Genesis, God said, "It is not good that the man should be alone; I will make [a] help meet for him" (Genesis 2:18). What do you think the word *help meet* means? According to *Strong's Concordance*, help meet means "a helper suitable for him."

Now that you know what a help meet is, you must understand and accept that being married is not about just you, your dreams, your goals, and your needs. In order for a wife to be an effective help meet to her husband, the woman must be the right match for the man who is to be her husband. Why? We are to help him by assisting him in every area of his life (e.g., keeping the home, praying for him, taking care of him and the children, building him, up just to name a few). The responsibilities of a wife are endless. Therefore, to marry a man without first consulting God and knowing the responsibilities of a help meet is foolish. Determining your true reasons for getting married will most likely stop many quick marriages that usually end in lengthy nasty divorces, which further casts a dim and disgusting view of marriage from the world's point of view.

Just as important as the question, "Should I get married?" is the question "Who should I marry?" You must understand that while God may have marriage in your future, it may not be with the person you want it to be. As a woman, you must understand that just because you spend months and years with a man does not guarantee marriage. He does not owe you a wedding ring, a wedding, a honeymoon, or a life of marriage just because you decided to invest your time, effort, money (and oftentimes body) into the relationship. Getting pregnant by him only guarantees that he is the father of your child or children, not your husband. When the relationship does not end in marriage, you just have to accept the fact that you made a long-term investment with no return.

Finally, if you know why you want to get married, you know that God desires for you to be married, and you are with the man that God wants you to marry, there is one last question. Is this the right time for you to get married? God works according to His own timetable, not yours or your fiancé's. You must know that by now. It does not mean that God has forgotten about your prayer request or your desire to be married. It just means that He needs you to wait for Him (God, not the man in your life) to finish preparing you both for marriage. When you marry in God's season, the man whom God has predestined to be your husband, you will have peace that passes all understanding (Philippians 4:7).

Personally Speaking

I want to share with you a time in my life when I too wanted to be married. It was many years ago. My reason was wrong because of my thinking. I've always compared my life to others: I didn't have enough education, I was too fat, I wore my hair to short; and the list just went on and on. Therefore, when a dear friend of mine was getting married after being widowed for a short time, I was upset and felt as though God was ignoring my request of marriage.

I was happy for my friend, but I was sad, too. The Word of God says in 1 Thessalonians 5:18-"In everything give thanks: for this is the will of God in Christ Jesus concerning you." I had lost sight of this scripture, but God soon provided me with the insight I needed. Well, as the wedding day approached, I angrily asked God why was I still waiting in line, and why didn't she have to wait. God did not answer my question, but He did tell me the following, "These women have to live with these men."

Once God put it that way, I decided I was not ready for marriage at that time in my life. You see, my desire to have a date to the wedding and not attend one more event without a companion by my side became my reason for wanting to get married. My "why?" was to not show up at an event without a man next to me—wrong reason!

Now my heart's true attitude and reason for getting married is this: if God can use me better as a married woman instead of a single woman to enhance His Kingdom and give Him glory, then I will marry the man God has predestined for me to marry in God's time. I will not manipulate a situation or second-guess a proposal because I know God will have guided both of our decisions to get married. How God can get the glory out of our lives should be the basis of all our decisions.

Bringing It Full Circle

When you think about getting married, your desire should be to marry in God's time the person God wants you to marry. Wanting God's best means doing it God's way. Marriage is too important to enter into it under circumstances other than those orchestrated by God.

If you truly want to be married, go to your prayer closet and pray like never before. Ask God if this is truly the lifestyle He has called you to live. If it is not and you marry anyway, you run the risk of mismanaging your marriage. If you mismanage marriage, you as a help meet have the potential to destroy two lives: yours and your husband's, and even more lives if you have children. I once took a class called Woman to Woman. One of the most important lessons I learned in that class was a wife could disqualify her husband for ministry simply by not being a wife who was in control of her actions. Therefore, if God's plan for your life is not for you to be married and you proceed anyway, you truly do run the risk of mismanaging the marriage.

Woman to Woman

I am convinced that many women are married and miserable simply because they did not ask why. They entered into marriage because someone other than God (e.g., family, friends, church family, church leaders, etc.) said it was the right move to make. Women were convinced that the men loved them and they loved them back. However, they never asked God if it was the right season, the right time, or the right man. Many of those women are divorced because they did not realize how much work is required to have a godly, healthy, happy marriage in an ungodly, compromising and lost world. No matter the reason we must not forget **Malachi 2:16, "I hate divorce, says the Lord God,"** Let me just say until I spoke to a pastor friend of mine, I thought I totally had this divorce and remarriage issue figured out, but it can be complicated. It is for this very reason I'm going to say God's intention was for all Christians to be married once for a life time. You'll need to study this out for yourselves starting in the Old Testament and in the New testament. I can tell you this, getting remarried is not as easy as we Christians are making it out to be. I also will say the scripture in 2nd Timothy 2:15 which states, "Study to shew thyself approved unto God, a workman that needeth not to be ashamed, rightly dividing the word of truth," has a new meaning to me. I would strongly urge you to study the word of God regarding the issues of divorce and remarriage. I believe if you are reading this book it's because you want to honor God with your life, and part of honoring God is being obedient in all areas even when it hurts and you don't quite agree or understand. God has never asked anyone of us to agree; he just wants us to trust Him and obey him. As Dr. Charles Stanley says and I quote, "OBEY GOD AND LEAVE THE CONSEQUENCES TO HIM."

I believe in my heart it's because of the paragraph above that God doesn't want another woman to marry out of duty, fear, or even a sense of responsibility to those seemingly in authority over her life. When a Christian woman or man marries, there is an absolute truth called the Bible that we're to live and abide by, so getting married may be easy but getting out of the marriage with God's approval is not that easy. Ladies, this is why I wrote this book in the first place; so that you'd be aware of the pitfalls. When you seek God on the front end of a matter, you don't have consequences; you have blessings. Your why for getting married can and will only be answered when you seek God for wisdom and guidance and then obey what God tells you. No one can tell you the plan God has for your life; therefore, seek God in this matter because your decision will have lifelong implications for you, your fiancé, and your children.

"Let us therefore come boldly unto the throne of grace, that we may obtain mercy, and find grace to help in time of need" (Hebrews 4:16).

Being Honest with God

1. Is this your season for marriage? If yes, how has God confirmed this to you? If no, what season does God have you in?

   _____

   _____

   _____

   _____

2. Is the man you want to marry the man God has told you to marry? If yes, how do you know?

   _____

   _____

   _____

   _____

3. If this is your season for marriage, and you are with the man God has chosen for you to be your husband, is it time for you two to marry?

_____

_____

_____

_____

4. Will you still trust and serve God if God's answer is no to question numbers 2 and 3?

_____

_____

_____

_____

Journaling with God

2

BEHAVIOR BEFITTING A GODLY WOMAN

Favor is deceitful and beauty is vain: but a woman that feareth the Lord, she shall be praised.

—Proverbs 31:30

Have you ever met women in the church who say they are a Christian, but the only thing that reflects a Christian lifestyle is that they attend Sunday service, Sunday school, and Bible study? I have met them, and at one time in my life, I was that woman. My walk did not match my talk, and my behavior was far from that befitting a professed woman of God. However, thanks to God's unconditional love, grace, and mercy, I am not that woman anymore.

I played Russian roulette with my life for a very long time. I did not know when I would take my last breath and stand before the Lord, ashamed! None of us know when that day will come because our lives are like a vapor (James 4:14). Yet, many women live their lives as though they have a lifetime to care about their testimony and the things of God. All the while, they are praying for God to send them a godly husband even though their talk, walk and lifestyle are far from godly. In fact, they believe that God will answer their prayer regardless of the ungodly and messy lives they live. You may be one of those women or you may know a woman like that. Well, I am here to tell you the answer from God is "NO!" God will not send you His best in a husband when you are not giving or living your best for God.

So, what is behavior befitting a godly woman? You attend church, you read your Bible, you pray with and for your friends on a regular basis. Is that not enough? It's a start, but that is definitely not where your walk with God should end. You see, your behavior is more than what you do. It is who you are and how you carry yourself as a woman representing God. Your conversations, attitudes, thoughts, and actions all indicate who you are, to Whom you belong, and where you are in your relationship with God.

Many Christian women are unrecognizable because their behavior outside the church is very different from their behavior inside the church, or at least inside the sanctuary. Instead of being a Sunday morning churchwoman, you must strive to be an everyday Christian woman. Second Corinthians 5:17 states, "Therefore, if any man [be] in Christ, [he is] a new creature: old things are passed away; behold all things are become new." Old things (including thoughts, actions, and speech) are to pass away when you become a Christian. The problem is that many people hold onto their old way of life and try to incorporate it into their new life in Christ. It is time to let go of your old life and Satan's lies that convinced you that nothing was wrong with that life. You cannot enter a new life freely and completely while holding on to the old.

Ephesians 4:22–24 states, "That ye put off concerning the former conversation the old man, which is corrupt according to the deceitful lusts; And be renewed in the spirit of your mind; And that ye put on the new man, which after God is created in righteousness and true holiness."

Let's also look at First Corinthians 6:9–11,

> Know ye not that the unrighteous shall not inherit the kingdom of God? Be not deceived: neither fornicators, nor idolaters, nor adulterers, nor effeminate, nor abusers of themselves with mankind, And such were some of you: but ye are washed, but ye are sanctified, but ye are justified in the name of the Lord Jesus, and by the Spirit of our God.

Ladies, the scriptures are very clear. Behaviors of the flesh should be a part of your past. Once you give your life to Christ, you no longer should be living a life of sin. A life free of sin is more than just avoiding sex outside of marriage. The Bible is clear that His people should abstain from all appearances of evil (1 Thessalonians 5:22). All means all. Ninety-nine point nine just won't do. This is why I am not just talking about premarital sex. This scripture refers to any behavior that can make a person question whether you are truly a Christian woman. Any behaviors that are not of God must be repented of immediately and not repeated (which is what true repentance requires).

First Thessalonians 4:4 says, "That every one of you should know how to possess his vessel in sanctification and honour." Godly women should be set apart in every way, from their wardrobe to their conversations to their associations.

Psalms 19:14 reads, "Let the words of my mouth, and the meditation of my heart, be acceptable in thy sight, O Lord." Even your thoughts have to honor God.

Colossians 3:8 reiterates, "But now ye also put off all these; anger, wrath, malice, blasphemy, *filthy communication* [emphasis added] out of your mouth." Control your tongue or it will destroy you.

After reading those scriptures, you may be asking how does one even begin to align their life with those scriptures? It depends on who you hang around. It is true that birds of a feather flock together. Who you associate with will affect what you wear, what you say, what you do, and how you do it. If you are around people who allow filth to come out their mouths, they will not mind when you curse. If your friends dress provocatively, they are not going to correct you when your skirt barely covers your underwear, your blouses reveal your cup size, and your dresses show where all of your curves curve. Who is going to say anything to you? No one will because birds of a feather flock together, which translates to a life and walk without accountability.

If you are going to live your life according to God's Word, you need friends who also desire to live by the same standard. You need friends who are not afraid or ashamed to hold you accountable to God's truth and tell you when you have detoured. "Faithful [are] the wounds of a friend; but the kisses of an enemy [are] deceitful" (Proverbs 27:6). They should also not mind you doing the same for them. They look out for your spiritual growth and development, and you help them with theirs. This is what the Word of God calls "iron sharpening iron" in Proverbs 27:17.

Living a godly life is not just for you. Your lifestyle is a testimony to the power of God being manifested in your daily walk. Titus 2:3 instructs that "the aged women likewise, that [they be] in behaviour as becometh holiness." You may not say that you are an aged woman, but the truth of the matter is, you are older than someone. Who is watching you? You do not know how many women are wishing they could be you. You have no idea what young woman or little girl has been watching your life and is willing to do anything to be just like you. Why? You have all the nice clothes. You seem intelligent. You drive a nice car and have a great job. Therefore, based upon outward appearances, she wants to be you—act, talk, and live like you. If given the chance, she will. She will do everything you do, and if you are living a sinful life, she will follow right after you. After all, you are a good Christian woman who would not lead her down the wrong path, or would you?

I was that young girl once upon a time, and it was a beautiful schoolteacher who took me under her wing. I wanted to be like her and dress like her. When she finished schooling me, I was having sex like her too. She said that as long as you loved a man, it was okay. She even said that her doctor told her she needed to be sexually active. Do not think for a minute that I did not take her story and make it mine, because I did.

It is our God-given responsibility to be a light to this dark dying world. Our relationship with Christ and our testimonies about that relationship should represent more than our church attendance, church membership, tithes, and offering. God does not need our money or church attendance. He needs women who are living their lives fully committed to Him in heart, mind, soul, and body because they love him. "And thou shalt love the Lord thy God with all thine heart, and with all thy soul and with all thine might" (Deuteronomy 6:5).

Woman to Woman

Ladies, your life should be an example for someone else, whether they are Christian or not. I would like to leave you with this scripture. If it affects you like it affected me, then praise God! After reading it, I pray that you will never look at your sin the same.

Ephesians 4:1 says, "I THEREFORE, the prisoner for the Lord, appeal to and beg you to walk (lead a life) worthy of the [divine] calling to which you have been called [with behavior that is a credit to the summons to God's service]." (Amplified Version)

Single Mom to Single Mom

If you are a single mom and have a daughter or daughters, I strongly urge you to live a life before your daughter or daughters that exemplifies a lifestyle of dedication and consecration to the Lord. Understand if you are engaging in sex outside of marriage, dressing provocatively, or having conversations that are not Christlike, please don't be surprised when she starts doing it also. She is taking her cues from you, and God will hold you personally responsible for her spiritual walk with Him. You and you alone hold the key to what she believes and knows about living a lifestyle committed to Him. Be selfless when it comes to her spiritual growth. I can't imagine anything more important than rearing a godly young woman to present to God.

After all, if you want God's best, don't you want her to receive God's best as well? She needs a mom, not a friend in you, and I'm not saying you shouldn't or can't be your daughter's friend. But what I am saying is being her mother comes first. Besides, she will meet enough girlfriends, but she only has one mom. Be all you can while you have time to impact her for our Lord. I told my daughter and son when they were young, "Your virginity and your relationship with God is my responsibility from age zero until you're eighteen. After that, it will be between you and God." Therefore, my main concern was that my behavior was that befitting a godly woman. I purposed in my heart to live a godly life before my children. We as single moms owe it to our children—girls and boys—to show them Christ in our walk as well as our talk. "Her children arise up and call her blessed" (Proverbs 31:28).

Being Honest with God

1. How do you live your life when no one is watching?

   _____

   _____

   _____

   _____

2. What behaviors do you need to change?

   _____

   _____

   _____

   _____

3. What associates and friends do you need to separate from?

   _____

   _____

   _____

   _____

4. What do you want people to say about your representation of God?

___

Journaling with God

3

Why Wait on God?

Wait on the LORD: be of good courage, and he shall strengthen thine heart: wait, I say, on the Lord.

—Psalms 27:14

In these times in which we live, everything moves at record speed. We are an instant gratification generation. We want everything now, now, now and have not the patience to wait for anything, not even God's answers to our prayers. Waiting for anything means you have to be still, especially when we want something so bad that we can see it (or so we think). We don't like waiting in lines, so we grumble and complain. We don't like waiting for promotions, so we quit our jobs. We don't like waiting for people to return our phone calls, so we text, e-mail, and instant message them just to say "hi." Waiting to checkout, eat, or talk is one thing. Waiting to get married is a whole other story.

For many women, waiting is not even an option, so they marry the first man that asks them. It is almost impossible for them to be still and wait on God for their chosen husband to find them. It does not help when we watch the scripted fairy-tale romances on television. How many of you are addicted to *The Bachelor* and *The Bachelorette*? We watch the show with the anticipation of someone finding true love. We watch them kiss, cuddle, make out, and spend the night together. We sit on the edge of our seats, so to speak, waiting to see who will get the final rose and then watch them embrace and declare their love for one another, only to find out that the couple broke up before the show even aired.

Now these are adults, and adults do what they want to do. However, if the young woman is a professed Christian, what do you think her testimony looks like now? Let's take it a step further. What became of her testimony when she arrived at the house and professed she was a Christian long before the show even aired? Her beliefs and convictions were questioned and smeared the very moment she submitted her name for consideration to even be on the show.

Shows, situations, gatherings similar to *The Bachelor* and *The Bachelorette* are just another example of women (and men) moving ahead of God. You may be asking, "Why wait on God?" My answer is "Why not wait? What's your rush?" If you want to be married, don't you think it's high time you get somewhere, sit down and be still with God? "Cast all your cares on Him, because He cares for you" (1 Peter 5:7).

Is waiting easy? No. Is being still easy? Double no. It is not easy for me to wait, just as I know it is not easy for you to wait. Nonetheless, if you want God's best like I do, you must wait on Him to do in your lives what you cannot do. God knows who the man is, where he lives, what he looks like, and the number of hairs on his head. God also knows if he is ready to be a husband to you and a father to your children (especially if you already have children), just as God knows if you are truly ready to be your chosen husband's wife and mother to his children, if he already has children.

Being still and waiting on God does not mean you do not desire to be married anymore. It is a very necessary process God uses to prepare us for marriage. We think we are ready because we are ready for the wedding and the honeymoon (which is big if you are a virgin or you have been celibate for a long time). However, when God finishes sifting and molding us into the women He created us to be, we will be emotionally, physically, mentally, financially, and spiritually prepared for marriage and all the responsibilities it bestows upon us. Isaiah 64:8 says, "But now, O LORD, thou [art] our father; we [are] the clay, and thou our POTTER; and we [are] the work of thy hand."

What does being still actually mean? It will mean different things to different women, depending on what God needs to do to prepare you for marriage. Now I can tell you what it does not mean: it does not mean sitting idle and twiddling your thumbs or watching paint dry. Being still is a form of waiting (i.e., waiting on others). Think of a waiter. A waiter serves others by providing a service, which is exactly what being still is all about. It involves being about your Father's business and occupying yourself until He comes. It entails working in ministry, serving in the local church, the community, or wherever God places you to serve in whatever capacity He assigns you. He may have you ministering the Word of God, singing in the choir, working with youth, or cooking in the kitchen. Whatever God has placed on your heart to edify the body of Christ, do it—and do it in a spirit of excellence.

This is also the time God is giving you to interact with Christian men in an appropriate manner and appropriate setting with appropriate boundaries. Whether it is a church, a community event, or other social gathering, these are opportunities for you to meet Christian men in a safe environment. You are not to make advancements toward anyone. Just be still and watch to see if God places anyone in your path and then pray about who is your path, and watch and see what God does; or see if God places a roadblock or red flag in your path. Your godly character will speak for itself and you. This is what will appeal to a godly man. As he observes your chaste conversation and feels the gentle nudging of the Holy Spirit, the right circumstances will bring the two of you together in God's time. God does not need your help! Please, repeat after me: *God does not need my help.* He just wants you to obey His Word regarding your godly character and behavior.

Notice that in the previous paragraph I did not mention work as an opportunity to make a possible love connection. I know many people have met their spouses at work; however, I personally do not believe that coworkers should date. My philosophy is, "Don't date your honey where you make your money." It can become complicated as well as messy, especially if there is infidelity, abuse, jealousy, or the relationship ends on other unpleasant terms. Yes, there are exceptions to the rule.

Just make sure God made it an exception and not either of you. If God does allow you to meet the love of your life at work that leads to marriage, you both will need to pray about whether one of you should find another job. It can create a financial strain on the marriage when both incomes come from the same employer.

When a woman (young or old) is waiting on God for marriage, it is important to stay focused on Christ, not yourself or the hundred prayers you send up to heaven for a husband. God is not forgetful. Trust me. He has heard every prayer you have ever prayed for everything you have ever prayed for and everything you have ever needed or wanted, and He is not going to forget the times you have spent beseeching Him for something as important as a husband.

Philippians 4:6 advises us to "Be careful for nothing; but in every thing by prayer and supplication with thanksgiving let your requests be made known unto God." Let's look at this scripture a little more closely. First, be careful for nothing. Do not fret or be anxious for anything, and that includes marriage! Why? An anxious decision is not a well-thought-out decision, and it will definitely not encourage you to wait on God. Have you ever noticed that it is the anxious, spontaneous decisions in life that have the most life-altering and costly consequences? How many situations are you still trying to overcome because you made decisions out of anxiousness and spontaneity? What have those decisions cost you?

The second part of Philippians 4:6 tells us to let our request be made known to God. God wants to be in every decision you make; therefore, He has instructed us not to be anxious but be prayerful. This is all a part of being still, which is why it is not easy living in a society of people who say you can have it your way, right now. This is the type of thinking that produces unplanned pregnancies, quick marriages, and quick divorces, that do not line up with the Word of God, not to mention incurable diseases. We must obey the scripture in 1st Thessalonians 5:21 which says "Prove all things; hold fast which is good."

Personally Speaking About Helping God Out!

Let me share with you a time in my life when I was anxious for love. How many of you have tried meeting someone on the Internet? Come on, be honest! Well, I have. I tried all the Christian dating websites and actually met someone. We talked for a long time on the phone until I found out he was cray to the z! (crazy!) as my spiritual grandson would say. He kept telling me that God told him I was supposed to be his wife. So I told him that when God tells me the same thing, we will get married. After some time, it became apparent that this telephone relationship was going nowhere fast, and he stopped calling. Thank you, God!

After that experience, it was clear that God did not want me meeting anyone that way. Well, did that stop me? Nope. I kept surfing the Internet looking for Mr. Right. In the midst of my disobedience, God protected me by not allowing anyone to contact me, absolutely no one! The men I was interested in dating were not interested in me, and those who were interested in me, I was in no way interested in them. I finally surmised that God did not want me using the Internet for that purpose, so I deleted my profiles. I also knew that, by what I was reading in the Word of God and discovering in my quiet times with Him, I was not going to meet my husband that way.

I am sharing this to show you how easy it is for us to get in front of God. The Internet, with all of its social networking sites (not to mention Twitter, chat rooms, and instant messaging), just makes it that much easier to move faster than God. Just like many women you know, I thought I would just help God. Then God reminded me, "Whoso findeth a wife findeth a good thing and obtaineth favor of the Lord" (Proverbs 18:22). After that, I knew I could not go back to looking for a husband on the Internet. I knew in my heart that God wanted my husband to find me, when my husband is ready to find a wife. However, as I continued to search the scripture, God showed me Proverbs 8:35: "Whoso findeth me findeth life, and shall obtain favor of the Lord." This was the scripture He'd written to me to seek Him, love Him, choose Him. One scripture is clearly written to men, and the other to women.

God wants to get all the glory. He has already chosen my husband, and in God's time my husband will find me. After all, I chose twice and got it wrong both times. Therefore, I am letting God choose because I know His choice will be the right choice, for God is *never* wrong!

Bringing It Full Circle

Since being still and waiting on God is a process, the whole process starts with our relationship with Christ. When God says, "Be still and know that I am God" (Psalms 46:10), will you obey God's Word or take matters into your own hands? What is your attitude toward what God has to say about getting married? Believe me. Your situation is unique and should be uniquely dealt with according to the Word of God. Your journey to marriage all has to do with God's plans for you, your husband, and the life you build together with God as your Architect.

Woman to Woman

Continue to be still, wait on God, and know in your heart that God has heard your petition for a husband. Therefore, you do not need to make another move in that direction until God says "Go!" Always remember that God does not need your help in finding a husband because he has already chosen him if marriage is His plan for your life. Because no good thing will he withheld from them who walk uprightly (Psalms 84:11). This means behavior befitting a godly woman.

Waiting on God means you trust His timing and His plan for your life, and this is the time that God is teaching you discipline in your life. This is also a precious time that you should be spending as much quality time as possible with God, getting to know Him and making Him your all in all, your everything.

Being Honest with God

1. How have you been waiting?

   _____

   _____

   _____

   _____

2. In your waiting period, what have you done to help God find you a husband?

   _____

   _____

   _____

   _____

3. What values and standards have you compromised in the name of love?

   _____

   _____

   _____

   _____

4. What can you do to be about your Father's business until you marry?

_____

_____

_____

_____

_____

_____

_____

_____

_____

_____

_____

_____

_____

Journaling with God

4

WHO IS YOUR ALL IN ALL, YOUR EVERYTHING?

And thou shalt LOVE THE LORD *thy God with all thy heart, and with all thy soul, and with all thy mind, and with all thy strength: this [is] the first commandment.*

—Mark 12:30

One morning, God spoke to my heart and asked me, "Who is your all in all, and your everything?" I had to stop and think. I started to say "You are, Lord." But before I could answer, He asked me, "How much time do you spend with me versus being on the Internet, watching television, or talking on the telephone?" I had to look at my walk versus my talk. Everybody that knows me knows that I love to talk. Even though many of my conversations are centered on God, His Word, His expectations of us, and the lessons He teaches us, that just is not enough. God wants me to desire to be with Him just as much as He desires to be with me. He wants me to spend more time with Him than those other things, including thinking about marriage.

Many times, we think God is our all in all. We say He is our everything; we attend church on Sunday, we teach Bible study, we sing in the choir, we drive the church van, and we sweep the church floors. Unfortunately, we can do all those things, and God will still not be on the throne of our hearts.

- What or who is the first thing you think about when you wake up in the morning and the last thing you think about before you go to sleep?
- Do you long to spend time in God's Word?
- Does God's will mean more to you than your or your pastor's opinion?

Oftentimes, we hang on to our pastor's words more than the Word of God to the point that if our pastor corrected God, we would agree with the pastor. We must be careful not to have anyone sitting on the throne of our hearts but the Lord Jesus Christ.

Cultivating our relationship with Christ is our most important relationship on this side of heaven. I know God wants to be everything to us because He tells us to love Him with our whole heart, soul, mind, and strength seventeen times from Deuteronomy to Luke! If you truly want that kind of a relationship with God, you have to work at it. Our flesh will do everything in its power to stop us from spending quality time with God. Satan will use every distraction to keep us from growing in our relationship with God. Satan will use television, phone calls, family, friends, and even writing a book to keep us from spending quality one-on-one time with God. Yes, writing a book to help women can be a distraction if it takes priority over my time with God.

If those things can distract you from your relationship with God, how much of a distraction will a man be? Do you know how difficult it is to cultivate two main relationships at the same time (e.g., maintaining a relationship with God and a relationship with your new boyfriend, fiancé, or husband)? It would be impossible. Someone would go lacking in their personal time with you, and I can tell you that it won't be the person you sleep next to every night or talk to every day. It would be the one you cannot see. That is why it is so vitally important to nurture and strengthen your relationship with Christ now by placing Him in His rightful place in your life. If you are dating someone, how much of your "My Time with God" gets placed on the back burner for "We Time" with the man in your life? Here's the kicker. Your boyfriend may not even know you are neglecting God for him, but you do by the choices you make when you answer his call, respond to his text, and read his e-mails when you are supposed to be praying, studying, or just listening to what God has to tell you.

Do you recognize the prompting of the Holy Spirit in your life? Do you know when He is urging you to act on something or refrain from doing something? You will as you begin to spend more and more time talking with God and studying His Word. Jeremiah 33:3 says, "Call unto me and I will answer thee and show thee great and mighty things which thou knowest not." All wisdom, knowledge, and understanding about God and His ways are in the Bible. Yes, God desires to be your all in all, but do you desire for Him to have that very special intimate place in your heart?

"There is difference [also] between a wife and a virgin. The *unmarried woman* careth for the things of the Lord, that she may be holy both in body and in spirit: but she that is married careth for the things of the world, how she may please [her] husband" (1 Corinthians 7:34).

With this scripture in mind, I understood that my season of singleness is not a burden but a beautiful time of training and transformation. It is a time to grow and get to know God as He teaches me how to be the woman He created me to be as I continue to serve God without distraction, as 1 Corinthians 7:35 states.

That is why this time in your life should be set aside just for you and God. You have always been everything to God. It is now time for you to do the same and become everything God needs you to become. Everything you need to know is in His Word. Allow Him to capture your mind and heart. This is the start of an amazing journey of knowing who God is as the Father, Son, and Holy Ghost in your life. Once your mind is set on making Him the number one priority in your life, this will be the beginning of a beautiful and everlasting relationship. Psalms 119:2 reads, "Blessed [are] they that keep his testimonies, [and that] seek him with the whole heart."

Bringing It Full Circle

Find a time just for you and the Lord to talk without any interruptions or distractions. This needs to be a time when you will not be answering the phone or looking at television. This is a time that you cherish and is off-limits to the rest of the world. In this scripture, wisdom is speaking, and she says the following in Proverbs 8:17, "I love them that love me; and those that *seek me early shall find me.*" Ladies don't you realize this is what we need, God's wisdom in our lives. God is waiting for us to seek him out and spend time with him. He has so much to share with us about ourselves, Him, and life. It is all in His Book!

There was a popular song entitled "I Miss My Time with You" by Larnell Harris. Here are just a few words of the song.

> [T]here he was just waiting,
> in our old familiar place
> an empty spot beside him,
> where once I used to wait
> to be filled with strength and wisdom
> for the battles of the day
> I would have passed him by again
> if i didn't hear him say

(Chorus)

I miss my time with you
those moments together
I need to be with you each day

Woman to Woman

Have you ever heard of the First Fruit Theory? Proverbs 3:9 states, "Honor the Lord with thy substance, and with the first fruits of all thine increase." While many people believe this scripture is talking about tithing (which it is), I also apply it to my time. Every morning that you wake up is a first fruit of your time for that day, and it should be given to God first. God always told the Israelites to give Him their best calf (without blemish) and their first harvest. Why? God wanted their very best just like He wants ours, and I believe this includes our time.

Do you realize that if you wait until evening to spend time with God, you've waited until the end of the day to find out what God wanted you to do throughout the day? In my personal life, I know that I experience the most problems on days I began my day without talking to God first. Giving God the firstfruits of your time is a key step to making God your all in all and your everything.

Being Honest with God

1. In a twenty-four-hour day, how much focused time do you spend with God?

   _____

   _____

   _____

   _____

2. When spending time with God, what things or people do you allow to distract you?

   _____

   _____

   _____

   _____

3. What boundaries can you set to protect your time with God?

___

___

___

___

4. List some ways that you can spend focused time with God.

___

___

___

___

Journaling with God

5

Prepare Ye the Way!

*The voice of one crying in the wilderness,
Prepare Ye the Way of the Lord, make his paths
straight.*

—Mark 1:3

"Marriage is a decision that should not be entered into lightly," says the pastor as he is preparing to marry a couple. Despite how many times men and women have heard those very words, marriage is still entered into lightly and hastily for reasons other than God's will. Too many women enter into marriage just because it seemed like the next logical step in the relationship.

We oftentimes long to get married but do not fully understand what marriage will cost us or even if we have what it will take to be a godly wife in our present state. Do you agree that for every assignment in life that God gives us, we must be prepared in some way? Well, marriage is no different. As a result, you must first and foremost prepare the way for Christ to come to you and prepare your heart and mind for marriage. There are so many unexplained, unasked, and unanswered questions about marriage that we need godly preparation for a season that should last a lifetime. "Till death do us part," remember? Also keep in mind **Malachi 2:16, "I hate divorce, says the Lord God"**

What does it mean to "prepare ye the way?" It means to create a favorable environment (e.g., lifestyle) that makes it easy for one to come to you. "Prepare ye the way" is another season of preparation that is twofold. It is (1) preparing ourselves to have a heart and life for God to come and prepare us to be the women God is calling us to be and (2) God preparing us for marriage. It is a process that allows God to prepare us to receive Him so that our relationship is one of growth. First Peter 2:2 states, "As newborn babes, desire the sincere milk of the word, that ye may grow thereby." Speaking of growth, what are you doing in your life to make you ready to receive your husband? Do you need to get rid of some girlfriends who are not sharpening you well? Maybe they are dulling your spiritual hearing so that you cannot hear the Holy Spirit clearly. Maybe you must leave your current church home because you have grown as much as you can there, and God must send you to a foreign land for further training and growth. Are you willing to go if and when God says "Go!"?

Prepare ye the way includes, but is not limited to, the following:

- Being open to the teaching God has for you as the type of woman you must be before God allows you to be a help meet. *Ruth's Task:* Was she willing to move to a foreign land and take care of her mother-in-law Naomi? *Esther's Challenge:* Would she still have a childlike faith and take instruction from her cousin Mordecai even after she was crowned queen? *Rebecca's Assignment:* Would she be the one watering the camels for Abraham's servant, or would she say, "Water them yourself, because that is too much work"? What would your responses have been?
- Obeying God and His plan for your life even when you do not know the outcome. Your willingness to obey could mean the difference between a marriage proposal and the dream of marriage.
- Changing your shallow thinking about his looks, his wardrobe, his job, his salary, his title, and his position in the church. None of these are indicators of a man's level of maturity in his walk with God and his spiritual character. Those things may be impressive, but when God teaches you what qualities you should be looking for in a husband, it will not be hard to know

him when you meet him; and believe me, looks will be the last thing on the list of godly attributes.
- Knowing, understanding, and accepting that your lifestyle, actions, and behaviors will impact your future husband's life within the home and his ministry, among God's people, just like his actions will affect yours.
- Training to understand the emotional, physical, spiritual, and even financial responsibilities of marriage. Allow mature women in all those areas to teach you how to search and study God's word concerning each area and then how to apply His truth in making responsible decisions. You may not want people in your business, but the Bible clearly assures that "there is safety in a multitude of counselors" (Proverbs 11:14). The knowledge you will gain from these women will help mold you into the woman God is creating you to be.

Notice that I said *women* (plural) and not *woman* (singular). That is because no one woman has all the experiences and wisdom needed in all those areas. Therefore, God will send the women He desires to mentor you and minister to your needs. You will have to be open to receive them because He very well may send someone you would not have chosen for yourself. This also makes you accountable to others, which is necessary in marriage.

Hebrews 5:12–14 states,

> For when for the time ye ought to be teachers, ye have need that one teach you again which [be] the first principles of the oracles of God; and are become such as have need of milk, and not of strong meat. For every one that useth milk [is] unskilful in the word of righteousness: for he is a babe. But strong meat belongeth to them that are of full age, [even] those who by reason of use have their senses exercised to discern both good and evil.

Many women are still drinking milk and should, in all reality, be eating meat, considering how long they have been in church. However, because they decided to skip a step or two in their spiritual walk with God, they have missed some very essential spiritual food. Although you should be farther along in your walk with Christ and possibly ready for marriage, you have actually been held back several grades by God because you have more to learn about being a godly woman before you can even begin learning about being a godly wife.

As the scripture explains, strong meat belongs to those who are of full spiritual age: mature women of God who can rightly divide the Word of truth and know their rightful place as Christian women in the church and in the home. Let's start with the basic spiritual thermometer of your readiness for marriage. If you do not think you can be submissive and do not agree with that scripture, then you are probably still drinking milk and are not ready for a marriage ordained by God to a man chosen by God.

Let's be honest. Even the most mature Christian women may not like the word submissive, but they know how to humbly respect and obey the word of God whether it makes them say "Amen!" or "Ouch!" Ladies, being submissive to Christ in your season of singleness will help prepare you to be submissive to your husband in your season of marriage.

On a deeper level, if you just refuse to be submissive to any male authority figure you might come in contact with whom God has placed in your life, you are still in the milk stages of your spiritual walk and will need the guidance, wisdom, and support of mature godly women who have learned to live out their lives according to God's Word. "Prepare ye the way" in this area of your life would be God assigning you to a particular mature godly woman and maybe even several women.

Woman to Woman

I believe that by living a life of preparation in everything you do, you will not only have the assurance that you are marrying the right man, but it will give him the assurance that he has found the right woman to be his help meet. Do not be afraid to allow God to show you who you are as a woman. Have the desire to let God make you into His very best, knowing that there is always work to be done in these fragile vessels that God has allowed His Holy Spirit to indwell.

Prepare ye the way to be the woman God has called you to be, knowing and understanding that only you can get in your way. We can only blame our failures on our upbringing, lack of knowledge, the devil, and our limited church teaching for so long. There comes a time in our lives when we have to take responsibility for our own actions or lack thereof. You can be the woman God has called you to be whether you are married or single. You just have to be ready to prepare ye the way for the Lord!

Being Honest with God

1. What women has God placed in your life to mentor you, and in what areas do they minister to you?

   _____

   _____

   _____

   _____

2. How well do you receive their counsel?

   _____

   _____

   _____

   _____

3. What habits do you have that could prevent you from being an effective help meet?

_____

_____

_____

_____

4. How will you allow God to change those areas of your life that do not represent Him?

_____

_____

_____

_____

Journaling with God

6

BYE-BYE BAGGAGE!

Brethen, I count not myself to have apprehended: but this one thing I do, forgetting those things which are behind, and reaching forth unto those things which are before. I press toward the mark for the prize of the high calling of God in Christ Jesus.

—Philippians 3:13–14

What's your baggage? Let's be honest. We all have some sort of baggage. Whether it is a carry-on bag or a ten-piece luggage set, you want to get married and have that wonderful wedding day followed by a forever-after love story. The wonderful news is that it is not impossible because with God all things are possible (Luke 18:27). It is possible to be healed of past hurts, past pains, and past loves gone wrong. However, in order to be healed, you first have to acknowledge that they even exist.

What baggage are you holding onto that may be preventing God from blessing you with the desires of your heart? We truly must search deep in our hearts for the answer to this question. Many times, we may have to go to God in prayer, asking him to show us those things that we are holding onto which may keep us from having the peace of God and experiencing all that He has for us. Psalm 139:23–24 instructs God to search us, "Search me, o God; and know my heart: try me and know my thoughts: And see if there be any wicked way in me and lead me into the way of everlasting." Ladies, we all have the ability to deceive ourselves; therefore, we must ask God to purge us. "Purge me with hyssop, and I shall be clean: wash me, and I shall be whiter than snow" (Psalms 51:7).

God wants to remove this baggage that we carry around in our lives that keeps us from experiencing all of the blessings He has for us. This baggage can come in many forms, and below are just a few.

The Trunk of Unforgiveness

You know this is your largest piece of baggage because it contains every offense ever committed against us since the day we were born that we can remember.

Unforgiveness does not come without blame. It also does not come with rights (the reasons that we feel are justified in our unforgiveness). Unforgiveness is basically our way of keeping people in their place within our lives by keeping score of what they did or did not do that offended us. It is a form of self-righteousness. Typically this is how it looks. We feel as though someone has wronged us. Not only did they not apologize, they did not even acknowledge that they did anything wrong. So until they come to us and give us this long spiel about how they hurt us, we will not forgive them. We will not release them from their unpaid debt.

Oh, we will talk to them and then talk about them, but we will not forgive them (which is why we still talk about them). What kind of godly character is this? There is absolutely no place in the believer's life for unforgiveness, simply because God has commanded us to forgive. "For if ye forgive men their trespasses, your heavenly Father will also forgive you. But if ye forgive not men their trespasses, neither will your Father forgive your trespasses" (Matthew 6:14–15). Do you want God to forgive you as you have forgiven others in your life? Well, He does!

This scripture reminds me that I do not have the right to withhold forgiveness. Forgiveness is not ours to own although we act like it. Forgiveness was a gift granted to all from the Cross. How can we withhold something that we ourselves daily so desperately need from God and others?

Yes, you have the right to feel disappointed, even angry. Your feelings were hurt. A friend or family member betrayed you, and you cannot see ever forgiving them. Well, I can tell you this. God does not ask if we want to forgive anyone. He tells us to!

Personally Speaking

Unforgiveness is very ugly on a woman, especially a professed born again Woman of God. I have experienced the pain of not wanting to forgive someone who had hurt me. Oh, how I carried that baggage around for a very long time. During this time, I desperately wanted to start a ministry for single moms. Please understand that I did nothing wrong other than harbor hatred and animosity against this woman because she truly had betrayed me. It got so bad that I would not even speak to her when I saw her at church. I was angry, and I wanted her to admit that she was wrong for what she did to me. If she didn't, then I decided that I was not going to forgive her offense. She needed to admit that she had wronged me. Well, my skewed way of thinking went on and on.

Believe me when I say I was bitter and was wearing it well. Everyone that saw my reaction toward her wanted to know what was wrong, and I had no problem telling them. Oh yes, in addition to being bitter, angry, and unforgiving, I was now a gossip and had the audacity to want to start a ministry.

Well, it took a really close brother in Christ to tell me that I had to forgive her. Not only did I have to forgive her, he told me that I needed to go to her and ask her to forgive me. What? Me, forgive her? Was he serious? Uh, why did I have to ask her to forgive me? I had not done anything wrong (except gossiped behind her back, hated her in my heart, and despised her very existence). I was mad!

You see, not forgiving her was not hurting her at all. It was hurting me. I had become an ugly representation of God, and it did not look good. My unforgiveness had become a root of bitterness, with its roots extending outward and attacking everything in its path. It was like a cancer. It infected one part of my life and then uncontrollably reproduced itself in other areas because I left it untreated, and even worse, fed it. My condition went from my feelings of being hurt to anger, to unforgiveness, and then hatred. It spread from my heart to my lips, which turned into bad-mouthing and gossiping.

I had a responsibility to stop it before it grew roots, but I didn't because justification became my cloak of self-righteousness. It gave me a false sense of validation and made me believe I had the right to feel and act in a manner unbefitting to a godly woman. I felt justified in my feelings because I would never treat someone that way. My self-righteousness and self-indignation took me further than her offense took her.

Over the years, I have learned that forgiveness is not for the other person; it is for me. There is healing in forgiveness. There is comfort, there is freedom, and most of all, there is Christ in forgiveness. I also had to understand that in asking her for forgiveness, she did not have to request it. I owed it to her, plain and simple. I did as my brother in Christ instructed. I asked her to forgive me, and she never even acknowledged that she had done anything wrong.

That was such a crucial time for me in my growth in the Lord. Was I going to renege on my responsibility to forgive her just because she did not ask me to forgive her? Oh, how I wanted to, but the Holy Spirit of God would not let me off that easy. I still had to say, "Please forgive me," and then name all the things for which I needed forgiveness. This was to set me free not her. She would have to deal with her own actions, and that was between her and God.

Ladies, if you did not receive any lessons from my personal testimony I just shared, then you are definitely not ready for marriage. Being a godly wife will require a lot of forgiveness up close and personal. As I mentioned before, women are excited about getting engaged and planning the wedding, but the wedding only lasts for a few hours in a day. It is the marriage that you will live day-to-day, month-to-month, year-to-year, decade-to-decade. For that reason, you must bring forgiveness to the marriage table, or you will most definitely find yourselves in marriage counseling or divorce court.

The Garment Bag of Pride

The garment bag carries our clothes that we do not want to put in our suitcase or carry-on bags. It preserves our suits, dresses, blouses, skirts, evening gowns, and any other outfits we don't want to get wrinkled. If you cover each outfit with a plastic dry-cleaning cover, it reduces the amount of wrinkles so your outfits will be sharp and eye-catching—just like your pride. We wear our pride just like we wear our clothes. Except pride takes away the beauty of our spiritual character and darkens the light of the Holy Spirit within us.

To be prideful means to be disdainful and haughty. Haughty is an adjective that means to think more highly of yourself than you ought to. Other words associated with being haughty are arrogant, insolent, lofty, high and mighty, and last but not least, prideful.

Pride results from the spirit of justification and self-aggrandizement (i.e., the act or practice of enhancing or exaggerating one's own importance, power, or reputation). Proverbs 16:18 warns that "pride [goeth] before destruction, and an haughty spirit before a fall." How does pride lead to destruction? Pride deceitfully convinces a person that they are self-sufficient, self-empowering, and self-sustaining, when in reality God supplies all of our needs and teaches us His Word, empowers us through His Holy Spirit, and keeps us by His grace and mercy. Pride places man's desires over God's will. God does not play second to anyone or anything, and no man takes credit for what only He can do. For this very reason, God detests a prideful spirit. Proverbs 16:5 warns that "every one that is proud in heart is an abomination to the Lord."

Do you think that a prideful woman is going to be a great help meet? Most men do not, and in the proving stages of your relationship, he will most likely end it if he discovers that this is one of your character flaws. Think about it for a moment. Why would a godly man marry someone who is an abomination to the Lord? Why would he marry someone who will be a stumbling block in his walk with God and hinder his prayers?

A prideful attitude means you always need to make your point. You have to be right all the time. Proverbs 27:15 compares a contentious woman with a continual dropping on a very rainy day. A prideful woman is argumentative and does not know how to control her tongue. Pride is a deadly quality that will destroy your relationships. It tears down instead of building up. It desires to have its own way instead of wanting the best for others. In its simplest form, it is selfishness, and there is no room for it in marriage as we learned in chapter 1. Read Proverbs 14:1 and see the contrast of the wise woman and the foolish woman. Remember, marriage is a life that is completely selfless. So yes, ladies, you will have to say goodbye to your garment bag of pride!

The Duffle Bag of Debt

How many of you have a duffle bag? If you don't have one, have you at least seen one? Well, it varies in size, but most duffle bags have plenty of extra pockets on all sides. The material is flexible so it easily expands when you stuff it full of stuff. It also has two hand straps and a long shoulder strap that adjusts for comfort and easy carrying, just like your debt!

Personal Debt/His and Yours

Your debt varies in amount, but there is your main debt like a car payment, student loans, or mortgage payment. Then you have these extra side pockets of debt like your credit cards that can bring with it late payments and high interest rates, which if not paid on time will cause your original balance to double, triple, and even quadruple. It has expanded beyond its initial size, just like a duffle bag!

Since your debt is tied to you personally, it goes wherever you go and into every relationship you have, including marriage. Financial problems have destroyed many marriages. If you believe marriage is in your future, then you need to get your financial affairs in order. Whether you talk about it or not, your debt will impact your marriage. To what extent depends on how much of it you eliminate before the wedding, which is also not a valid reason for increasing your debt. If you cannot totally eliminate your debt, then at least get it to a point where it is manageable. Romans 13:8 states, "Owe no man anything but to love him."

By the same token, I would not recommend marrying a man who has a great deal of debt because his debt will become your debt (and vice versa). How can this happen if your name is not on his bills? Well, money spent on personal debt leaves less money available for household and childcare expenses. When the basic needs for the household and children cannot be met, it creates a strain on the marital relationship.

How do you find out his financial status? You ask the hard questions.

- Do you have any credit card debt?
- What is the combined total of all credit cards owed? What is your average combined monthly payment for credit cards only?
- What is your credit score? Can I see a copy of your most current credit report?
- Do you have any student loans? How much?
- Have you defaulted on any loans?
- Have you ever filed for bankruptcy? If so, when and why?
- Do you owe back taxes? If so, how much and why?
- Have you ever not filed taxes?
- Do you owe your family and friends any money? How often do you borrow money from them?
- Do you pay alimony?
- Do you pay child support?

By the way, before you ask him those questions, you might want to do a self-examination of your own financial status with the same questions (and yes, there are women who have to pay alimony and child support). I know for some of you this will be a big task. For others, you have already begun the process. Wherever you are in this process of being debt-free,

I advise you to not give up. Continue to ask God to help you curtail your spending and teach you how to be a good steward of the finances with which He has blessed you. We serve a wonderful, loving, and awesome God, and He will show you the way to financial freedom and stability if you are sincerely ready to follow Him and trust Him.

Credit Scores

You need to know his credit score. If his credit score is below six hundred, then major purchases (home or car) and even routine purchases (cell phones) will have to be obtained through you (that is, if you have a decent credit score). Low credit scores will also limit one's ability to obtain employment in certain professions. Based upon his answers to the above questions, you may not need to see his credit report.

As always, when you ask him these questions, you need to make sure you are prepared to answer them yourself. First Corinthians 14:40 says, "Let all things be done decently and in order." Make sure your financial house is in order before you start inspecting his financial house. If it is going to take time to eliminate your debt, at least be able to present a plan of action on how you are going to do so. This plan should also include how you are going to pay back your personal debt if you lose your job or cannot work due to pregnancy or other unexpected circumstances.

Marital Money Management and Finances

Once you and your fiancé have discussed both of your financial statuses, the next conversation should be about marital financial management. Due to the current economy and job market, it is recommended that families learn how to live on one income (preferably the husband's since he is the head of the household and the provider). If you choose to work, both of you need to decide whether your money will be used for other family expenses (i.e., vacations, savings, investments, emergency funds, etc.).

Even if the two of you decide to share the financial responsibilities for the basic household and childcare expenses, there still needs to be a discussion and agreement on how that will look. Some of the questions to discuss include, but are not limited to:

- Who will manage the checkbook? This should be the person with the better money management skills.
- Will you have just one joint account? Will you have two personal accounts, or will you have both?
- How will money be spent from the joint account? Will you both have debit cards?
- What types of purchases must you discuss before making them?
- How will you handle requests for money from family and friends?

- How will you handle borrowing money from family and friends?
- Who will make sure the household bills are paid either by check or online?
- Will you work while pregnant or after you have children?
- If you work, will they be in day care, or will a friend or family member keep them?
- If you both work, will you take turns staying home if the children cannot go to day care or school?

The Entrepreneurial Visionary

This is the man who has his own business and is his own boss or dreams of being his own boss. I will be the first to say that building your own business is an awesome career choice, especially if God has ordained it. Just do not get ahead of God in its implementation. If you are marrying an entrepreneur or aspiring entrepreneur, you will need to find out the following:

- Does the business make enough money to cover the business expenses?
- Does the business make enough for him to earn a salary that provides for his basic needs and routine expenses (e.g., housing, utilities, food, clothing, gas, auto maintenance, emergencies, etc.)?

- Is he willing to work a job while building his business, or does he believe he needs to commit 100 percent of his time to his business venture?
- Does the business have any debt?
- Is the company a limited-liability company?
- If his business profits decrease, what is his plan to supplement his income?

These are just a few questions you need to ask, so feel free to ask more. The more you discuss these things in the beginning, the easier it will be to trust one another as you begin building a future together. His answers may also tell you if there are any risks of financial abuse. Ask the questions, hear his answers, pray and wait for God to tell you how to proceed.

As an individual and as a family, you must find balance in spending and saving. It will save your marriage and future heartache and pain. God wants us to have nice things, but He also wants us to be wise with our finances. Here's a simple way:

- Pay God first with your tithes.
- Pay yourself the same amount in a savings account.
- Deposit a portion into the emergency fund (even if it is just $10.00 per paycheck).
- Pay your bills.
- In your budget, you should always have a petty cash amount. This is money that you get to spend on what-

ever you want. This is your fun money, whether it is $20 or $200. If you have more month than money, start saving a petty cash fund with what you have and then build up.

God is the best financial planner you will ever need. Seek Him in this area for you and your family, and He will equip you with the tools, knowledge, and wisdom to build a solid financial future. Be faithful with His blessings and remember that our financial blessings are not just for us, but also for the building up of His Kingdom. Take care of your business so you can take care of His business.

The Extra Bags of Childhood and Family Traumas

This topic alone could be a book. Therefore, due to the extensive nature of this topic, I will only encourage you to seek professional help if you have suffered any childhood or family traumas throughout your life. These traumas can range from parental abandonment or neglect, to physical, spiritual, emotional, or sexual abuse (including rape), to the incarceration or death of one or both parents. This can also include situations where your mother and/or father failed to protect you from situations because they either did not know you needed protection while visiting family and friends, or they did not believe you when you told them.

You must understand that no matter how much your fiancé loves you, he is not your counselor. Even if he is a licensed Christian counselor, he does not need to be your counselor. Men love to fix things and people. Childhood traumas are not "fix its." They require the proper support system in order for you to begin the healing process so the memories and scars will not jeopardize the future that God has planned for you.

Also, before sharing information about family issues or childhood traumas with your fiancé, pray and ask God if this is information you should be sharing. Remember, if you chose him and not God, there is a very good chance that the relationship will not last. Therefore, he is definitely not someone you want to divulge such intimate information. Do you really want someone whom God did place in your life to have that kind of information within their possession? Even if God did choose your fiancé, you still need to pray and ask God to present the best opportunity to talk to your fiancé.

The Junk Closet of Procrastination

You know the closet, the one with the unopened boxes, unfinished projects, old clothes and shoes that need to be donated, unfiled papers, unread books (including the Bible), keepsakes from old loves, and unpacked bags from your last trip. You may not have a junk closet, but maybe you have a junk drawer that contains your unopened mail, unpaid bills, unwritten thank-you notes, and old lists of things to do that never got done because you couldn't find the list. Whether it is a closet, drawer, or storage bin, it does not matter. All of these things are indicative of one issue: procrastination, the inability to follow projects to completion, or just plain laziness.

In this society, it is easy to get caught up in the mundane tasks of daily living: working, cooking, cleaning, grocery shopping, running errands, and doing laundry (especially if you already have children). We get caught up in the routines of life, and dismiss any thoughts about doing another thing like studying our Bibles, taking care of our health, organizing our homes, and spending time in prayer. Well, the junk closet has a name, it's called *procrastination* or *laziness*, depending on which term makes you feel better. The Bible characterizes a person with this trait as a sluggard. Proverbs 13:4 says, "The soul of the sluggard desireth and [hath] nothing: but the soul of the diligent shall be made fat."

In the space below, make a list of unfinished projects just from last year:

- _____
- _____
- _____
- _____
- _____
- _____

- _____
- _____
- _____
- _____

I pray you did not need extra lines. How many unfinished projects are there for the past five years or even ten years? Learn to finish what you start, and your list will not be so long. When you accept this life motto, you will also be a lot more selective in the things you start. This type of thinking reduces the chances of you making anxious or spontaneous decisions as we discussed in chapter 3, like beginning and ending relationships without consulting God first.

Let's look at some common areas that we as women tend to neglect for one reason or the other:

- **Our Prayer Life.** I believe many Christians struggle in this area because it can be done anywhere: in the car, lying down, driving, putting on makeup, or even cooking meals. We know we can talk to God anywhere at anytime, but prayer should be more than that. It is about having a focused, uninterrupted conversation with God.

We also tend to approach our time with God as gimme-time with Him. You know, give me this, give me that. We should always approach the throne of God with thanksgiving and reverence. If we truly considered what was given up for us to have complete access to the throne of grace, our attitudes surely would change. "And Jesus cried with a loud voice, and gave up the ghost. And the veil of the temple was rent in twain from top to bottom" (Matthew 15:37–38). The shed blood on Calvary was the payment rendered by Jesus for us to have direct access to the throne of God. Every time you talk to God, do you realize that you are standing on holy ground? As a result of Christ's dying on the cross, we have the ability to leave the natural and enter into the spiritual realm through prayer.

Even though we can talk to God whenever we want to, we should still set a time when we meet with Him to thank Him, praise Him, and reverence Him. This should also be time for you to just be still and listen to what He wants to tell you. It is time to say good-bye to a good night or table-grace prayer life and move into a prayer life that moves mountains and changes lives. You will see a new you when you learn to see prayer as a time of praise and worship and not a time of gimme and woe is me. This is the type of prayer life that is required for marriage.

- **Our Physical Health**. Our body is the temple of God, and we should be treating it that way. The older we get, the more susceptible we are to health risks. We do not schedule enough routine medical and dental examinations. This is what helps our doctors and dentists determine potential medical problems in the early stages. Most serious medical conditions can be avoided if we would just schedule our precautionary medical visits instead of waiting until there is a problem. In reality, by the time the problem manifests itself into detectable symptoms, there has been a problem for an extended period of time already.

Knowledge of your family medical history is a must. I realize this can be a challenge, if not impossible, if you never met your mother or father. However, if you do know them or other relatives, you need to research both sides of your family tree. My mom died at sixty-four and my dad died at age sixty-five. Since I have both of their genes, I realize that I am prone to every disease and medical condition they had. This was a wake-up call to me and has made me very aware of my health.

At a minimum, you should see your doctor at least once a year. These precautionary practices need to continue after you are married and have children. No one is going to take care of you like you will. You want to be healthy for your husband, your children, as well as yourself.

- **Our Weight**. A key part of treating our bodies as the temple of God is maintaining a healthy weight (not too big, not too thin). If you are overweight, you need to lose weight. If you are too thin, you need to gain weight.

Remember that as we get older, our bodies are changing every day. We have to learn to adjust to the body God gave us and take care of it to the best of our abilities from the inside out. Both of which should be done under the care of your physician. Unhealthy weight sizes affect your immune system, organs, and the overall body's ability to function at top performance.

- **Our Physical Appearance.** Do not ever leave your house in your pajamas, rollers in your hair, and slippers on your feet. There is an appropriate attire for home and an appropriate attire for every place else. You are a representative of God and should always represent Him, looking your best. I have two main tips for looking nice: dress your size and dress your age. If you are a size 16, do not wear a size 10. If you are forty-five years old, do not dress like a twenty-two-year old no matter how physically fit you are. Men want to see a woman who is well put together and does not have to show everything God blessed her with just to feel attractive. Ladies, less truly is more.

- **Our Homes.** Do you have a cluttered or messy home? If this is a habit of yours, it is time to find a better habit. Most men, no matter how messy they are, do not want to come home to a dirty or cluttered home. If there is junk in it, clean it up, go through it, organize it, discard what's old and useless, and find a place for the things you need to keep. In order to live the life God has for us, we must get organized and stay organized. God said it is our job to be keepers of the home in Titus 2:5. Enough said.

Bringing It Full Circle

We must learn to be diligent in all that God has laid at our feet. Marriage is too important to enter into lackadaisically. It must be entered into with prayer, purpose, and passion. Being married is a lifelong commitment to be all you can be for each other, your children, and the Kingdom of God. That is why saying goodbye to those things that will cause a stumbling block is very important.

Being Honest with God

1. Who do you need to forgive and for what?

   _____

   _____

   _____

   _____

2. How has pride affected your ability to lead a life completely submitted to God?

   _____

   _____

   _____

   _____

3. In what areas of financial stewardship do you need to improve?

   _____

   _____

   _____

   _____

4. What unfinished projects do you have, and what is your plan for completing them?

_____

_____

_____

_____

5. Write down your self-care schedule that provides time for you to nurture your relationship with God and take care of yourself?

_____

_____

_____

_____

Journaling with God

7

CLOSING STATEMENT

*Let another man praise thee, and not thine own
mouth; a stranger, and not thine own lips.*

—Proverbs 27:2

Life is a journey, is it not? It has seasons, and you will encounter tests, trials, or temporary assignments that God will allow you to experience. What will be said of you at the end of these tasks? Will it be said that you ran a good race, a fair race, a godly race?

What would God say about your past relationships? If the relationship ended abruptly, would it be said that you were a godly woman to the very end, or could words be used to describe your behavior and attitude as behavior less than befitting a godly woman? How did you end the relationship or allow it to end? What would be your closing statement?

Every journey has a beginning and an ending. "To every (thing there is) a season, and a time to every purpose under the heaven" (Ecclesiastes 3:1). How you enter and exit these seasons in your life will often indicate how you will handle your season of marriage. God requires us to handle situations decently and in order according to 1 Corinthians 14:40. In the previous chapter, I talked about leaving the past behind, but we cannot really leave it behind until we have dealt with the issues that those relationships created. Although we are not responsible for other people's actions, we are responsible for ours, and how we close the doors to our past will definitely affect our ability to move toward our future.

Ladies, let's face facts. Relationships end, and we sometimes get hurt in the process, but ladies, men get hurt too. What we do with these heartaches will help shape who we are as godly women. Therefore, closing the door appropriately and in a manner befitting a godly woman is very important to our testimony and our spiritual growth.

You may ask what in the world does this have to do with being a help meet. It has everything to do with it. Would you consider drinking spoiled milk? No, you would throw it out and get a brand new carton of milk. It is the same concept when starting a new relationship with spoiled hurts or a spoiled (i.e., broken) heart. You cannot love completely again until you have healed completely, and you cannot do that if the past doors are not closed properly and sealed shut.

That is definitely easier said than done. If you are like many women (and men), you do not always close the door to old loves right away or even completely. Too many times, you leave it cracked open just in case things change. It could be that you still love him, and maybe if you pray hard enough, God will make him love you back. My sisters, you cannot even begin to move in the direction of marriage if you are still in love with someone else. Unfortunately, many women do it and then do not understand why they are having problems in their marriage. You cannot share your heart with your husband if your ex-boyfriend still has it in his hands.

Then, there is the scenario where you ended the relationship. Now, you are second-guessing your decision and praying that he will take you back. You will not always have the chance to undo something or take back a decision. That is why, again, it is so crucial that you do not make anxious or spontaneous decisions based on emotions or partial information. Let's be honest. As women, we have a bad habit of making a whole story out of half the facts. In this situation, fear has set in—fear that we will not meet anyone else—and so we keep the door cracked just in case. In other words, you do not trust God to provide His best for you. Even if God's best is Himself, is that not better than being in a relationship that doesn't make you feel special, loved, and protected, or staying in a relationship that God has clearly said should end?

Even if God reveals to you that you should not have ended the relationship, there is no guarantee that the man you walked out on will accept you back into his life. I believe it is harder for men to open themselves up again to a woman who has hurt them. The moral of this story is when you go to close the door on a relationship, make sure the door is supposed to be closed. If not, the other person just may lock it and throw away the key.

Finally, you may not love your boyfriend anymore. It happens. However, he stills loves you, so you string him along just so you can brag to your girlfriends about how he can't get over you. Leaving someone's heart and mind in the balance to figure out what is going on in the relationship is mean and selfish. Humiliating another person, especially when they are opening their heart to you, is a clear sign that you are not ready for a new relationship, let alone marriage. Why? Marriage is a lifetime of selflessness. Luke 6:31 admonishes, "And as ye would that men should do to you, do ye also to them likewise." In other words, do unto others as you would have them do unto you. Treat people the way you want to be treated because you will reap what you sow. Galatians 6:7 says, "Be not deceived; God is not mocked: for what soever a man soweth, that shall he also reap."

Regardless of whether the issue is pride, unforgiveness, or both, you need to deal with it. Some women are controlling. They have to know how the relationship will end, or they will not invest in it. So they have one foot in the relationship, and one foot out the door until God shows them what is on the other side. Even though God has told you to end the relationship, you will not do it. Not only do you have trust issues, you are disobedient as well. Remember, obedience is better than sacrifice. Until you obey God's will, you will be waiting until Jesus returns before God will show you anything. It is called faith. Without it, it is impossible to please God. (Hebrews 11:6)

Personally Speaking

I remember when I was married and I wanted my marriage to work. I did everything in my power to make it work. I wanted love, and he wanted out, arguing that we married too quickly. I had to learn a few things about love:

- You cannot make someone love you no matter how hard you try.
- You cannot make someone stay when he wants to leave.
- You cannot keep a man who does not want to be kept.

Nevertheless, the Holy Spirit kept telling me to pray "Let Your will be done." I would not pray that prayer because I was afraid that God would let my husband leave me. I was holding on to him by praying, "God, make him love me. Work our marriage out." I fasted. I prayed. I cried. I did it all, but nothing changed how he felt about me or our marriage.

Finally, in my desperation to get spiritual, emotional, and physical relief, I surrendered to God's will and prayed, "Lord, let Your will be done!" There! I had prayed with my whole heart, now what? What would happen to me? What would happen to my marriage that I desperately wanted. Well, it ended. I came home one day, and he had moved out. He didn't just move out of the house; he moved to a different state.

At that point, I needed to let go completely and allow God to heal me. It still took a while because I did not want to close that door. What I did not understand was that the door was already closed. When a person does not love you, the door to their heart is closed, and there is nothing you can do to open it. There is no relationship. If you insist on having this relationship, you will most definitely be hurt and more than likely humiliated. When God told me it was over and to close the door, I should have heeded His direction. Although I was sad and hurt, I got through it with God's grace and mercy, and my children survived with little to no scarring, and for that I am thankful.

This is another reason why it is important to wait for God and marry the man that God has chosen for you. A man chosen by God will love God more than he loves you. For it is his ability to lead a completely submitted life unto God that will help him honor his wedding vows and be the man, husband, and father that God has called him to be. Please know that this does not mean he will not stumble or fall; however, it does mean that he knows there is a throne of grace that is available to him when he chooses to approach it.

Bringing It Full Circle

Your desire to be a help meet and getting that request granted or denied by God could very well hinge on your obedience to close doors in your life appropriately the first time, or to go back and assess if the door should have been closed in the first place. Being obedient in either of these situations will indicate your level of commitment to becoming the help meet to the man God has chosen for you. Now remember, obedience is what is important, not the outcome. You will never know if it was just a test.

In Genesis 22, God tempted Abraham by requesting that Abraham use Isaac as a burnt sacrifice. Abraham did not hesitate and was obedient. He trusted God to provide a sacrifice, and he loved God enough to sacrifice his only son! When will you love and trust God enough to obey? Your closing statement will mean more than your need to get even, your fear of not having someone in your life, or your desire to hold on to someone you still love who does not love you. All you know is that the door must be closed, and it must stay closed if you are going to become God's best in order to receive God's best.

Woman to Woman

Closing doors does not mean it is the end of life as you know it; it could mean it is the beginning of something beautiful, something perfect, something wonderful, and something ordained by God. However, you cannot and will not get there until you trust God and close all doors the right way in the right time. We are so anxious we get ahead of God in starting relationships, and we get ahead of God in regard to ending relationships. God told us to sit in the backseat, but we took control of the car and told God to move to the backseat with our haughty "I got this" attitude. Then what we have is a mess caused by our prideful disobedience. Either God is in control or you are. Which one is it? You will have to answer that question for yourself. Whatever the answer is, God knows the truth, and every one else will know when the outcome shows itself. You can fool some of the people some of the time, and you can fool some people all of the time, but you can't fool God at all. Remember that!

Will it be easy to close the door? No, it will not, but it will be worth it! James 3:17 says, "But the wisdom that is from above is first pure, then peaceable, gentle, and easy to be intreated, full of mercy and good fruits, without partiality, and without hypocrisy." Remember, to obey is better than sacrifice; close the door with love, grace, and mercy. Most of all, do not forget to say "Goodbye, and I will be praying for you." What a godly woman you are when you can wish him well and mean it in your heart. Why not? God has a wonderful life waiting for you on the other side.

Being Honest with God

1. What relationships have you ended, and why?

   _____

   _____

   _____

   _____

2. What relationships were ended by your boyfriend or Fiancé, or ex-husband and why?

   _____

   _____

   _____

   _____

3. What physical or emotional connections do you still have with your former loves?

_____

_____

_____

_____

4. If God has someone new for you, how will you close the doors to your prior relationships that you believe you cannot live without?

_____

_____

_____

_____

Journaling with God

8

Holiday Heartburn

This is the day which the Lord has made;
we will rejoice and be glad in it.

—Psalms 118:24

I have talked about waiting on God, closing the doors to past relationships, and preparing ourselves for the husband God has for us. With all of that being said, I am not going to minimize the fact that waiting is still very difficult. There are days and events in our lives that make waiting more difficult to face than others. For me, it is the holidays. I call it my "holiday heartburn."

Personally Speaking

Not every holiday is difficult for me, and the holidays that are difficult for me are not the same holidays that may be difficult for you. Why? Holidays mean different things to different women; therefore, your holiday heartburn may be for a different holiday than the two I am going to share with you.

The two holidays that are the most challenging for me are New Year's Eve and Valentine's Day. I believe New Year's Eve is difficult because it represents bringing in a new year, a new season of life. As far as relationships are concerned, I am not bringing a new relationship, or old one for that matter, into a new year. I am entering the new year just like I left the last year—as a single woman with no husband, no fiancé, no boyfriend, and no date! Thus, every year when New Year's Eve approaches and I am not in a relationship, it brings heartburn to me, and I am saddened that I am still waiting.

Valentine's Day is a little different. With New Year's Eve, I do not have to be with other couples. I can stay home and lick my wounds, so to speak. However, with Valentine's Day, I am usually at work watching flowers, balloons, and gifts being delivered to girlfriends and wives. At the end of the day, I am not anyone's valentine. Oh, how that heartburn hurts.

Let's Break It Down

We have feelings, and if we are going to get through the holidays successfully, then we must acknowledge which holidays bring us heartburn and why. Again, we must know our *why*. Then we have to create a plan to get through those holidays without being miserable and making some life-altering mistakes that may cost us God's best.

When you are experiencing holiday heartburn, your thinking is not very clear, if at all. This is a time of pain. You are unhappy because God still has not provided what you desperately want (or think you want). Since this is a vulnerable time, holiday heartburn must be taken seriously and requires that you take your holiday heartburn antacid. How do you do that?

Step Number 1

Find out which holiday makes you the saddest and makes you long for love. Whichever holiday triggers those types of emotions is your holiday heartburn. I believe knowing which holiday creates your holiday heartburn is the first antacid tablet you have to take because it is the first step in acknowledging that there is a problem.

Step Number 2

Pray and ask God for a plan that will help you get through that holiday with the least amount of pain and heartache. Matthew 7:7 states, "Ask, and it shall be given you; seek, and ye shall find; knock, and it shall be opened unto you." Knowing that God hears our prayers is different from believing God hears our prayers and will answer them. How? Knowing and believing are two different matters. Knowing involves your mind, but believing involves your heart. This is where your faith comes in. Hebrews 11:1 explains it this way, "Faith is the substance of things hoped for and the evidence of things not yet seen."

God is a loving Father, and He does not want His children hurting. Many times, our longing for love is overwhelming because we refuse to include God in our feelings. We want to wallow in "woe is me" time. That is okay as along as you do not allow those feelings to take you to a place or make a decision that will cause you to disobey God (i.e., to sin).

Step Number 3

Plan your time wisely for that day. Decide what you enjoy doing the most and spend your time doing that. Be careful because the enemy will definitely attack when you are not looking. Have you ever heard the old saying, "An idle mind is the devil's workshop?" Well, I am telling you that most of my problems resulted from me not following 2 Corinthians 10:5 and not "casting" down imaginations, and every high thing that exalteth itself against the knowledge of God, and bringing into captivity every thought to the obedience of Christ."

Philippians 4:8 also comes to mind. "Finally, brethren, whatsoever things are true, whatsoever things are honest, whatsoever things are just, whatsoever things are pure, whatsoever things are lovely, whatsoever things are of good report; if there be any virtue, and if there be any praise, think on these things."

Wow! God's Word just instructed us on how to handle holiday heartburn! Instead of thinking about what we do not have, think about all we do have. We all have something for which to be thankful. We all have something for which we can praise God.

Approaching your Holiday Heartburn Day can and may cause some anxiety for you! I stated earlier you should begin planning how you will spend that holiday so as not to be a victim of its pitfalls. However, in experiencing a recent holiday heartburn day myself, I must also warn that although you may be planning what you believe to be a cautious and careful day, be prepared to change your plans when the Holy Spirit prompts you to do so.

This is how we should treat all of our holiday heartburns: Yes, seeing the truth of our situations hurts, but praising God for getting us through it. Thinking on the things in Philippians 4:8 will no doubt make this process easier.

Personally Speaking, Again

It is imperative that you obey the prompting of the Holy Spirit since God is always right, and you are always wrong. Let me share my most recent holiday heartburn story with you.

It was New Year's Eve, 2011. As Christmas approached, I knew that New Year's Eve would be here. Since I'm aware that New Year's Eve is one of my holiday heartburns, I did not want to get caught off guard. Therefore, I decided that

I was not going to sit at home one more New Year's Eve. I thought if I'm going to bring the New Year in again alone, then I'm going to do it in style. So in early November, I booked myself a room at a really nice hotel. I decided I would purchase some of my favorite foods and an expensive bottle of sparkling cider. I would take my Bible and study material with me and bring in the New Year that way. My thought was at least I would not be at home. Well, how many of you know that our thoughts are not God's thoughts?

I asked my daughter if I stayed at the hotel would she take me and pick me up. I don't like parking garages, especially when I am by myself. See? I was being proactive here! She knew where I was, so I thought this would somehow protect my testimony. I shared my plans with only a few friends.

Little did I know that God had another plan for me. As the time got nearer, the Holy Spirit spoke to me and said you can't stay at the hotel on New Year's Eve! Well, I said, "Oh yes, I can!" I was not about to stay home and that was all there was to the matter! Again, I felt this strong urge from the Holy Spirit saying you cannot stay at the hotel, cancel your reservations. Given everything *I* had done to be proactive and protect my testimony, I questioned God as to why I had to cancel my reservations, and the Holy Spirit said, "Abstain from all appearance of evil" (1 Thessalonians 5:22).

Although I did not want to, I knew in my heart I had to cancel *my* plans. I was very upset, not to mention depressed and angry. Why did everything in my life have to be so difficult? Why couldn't I be like so many other single women who are free to do what they want, when they want, and how they want? I wasn't going to the hotel to have sex. I wasn't going to meet a lover. I just did not want to stay home alone again!

Needless to say, God had the last word, and I canceled my reservations, but not before I was told by others that I did not need to or have to cancel my reservations. I was told by a well-meaning Christian woman that my decision not to go to the hotel was over-the-top. Let me say this: She was not trying to give me the wrong advice. She just wanted me to be happy and did not want to see me sulking because I was alone again. She knew my testimony and had no reason to believe that me staying at a hotel could cause a problem.

However, this is where it is imperative that you yourself have an intimate relationship with God because people are not always going to agree with how *you* protect *your* testimony! My decision not to go may have seemed over-the-top to her and possibly even you, but was it really? I am a licensed minister of the gospel. How would I have looked leaving a hotel on New Year's Day? What accusations could have been stirred up? Understand this, when I got the advice that I did not have to cancel my plans and I should go, the Holy Spirit said, "We ought to obey God rather than men" (Acts 5:29). At that point, it was settled in my heart and mind that I was not going.

I also shared this story with my pastor. In his godly wisdom, he shed more light on this seemingly innocent situation. He stated that while, yes, I needed to avoid the appearance of evil, maybe God was protecting me from unseen danger. He shared that what if someone noticed me at the hotel alone and attacked me and left me for dead in some hotel room? Ladies, my thoughts had never even taken me that far. I just had not thought it out like that. However, God had and not only wanted to protect my testimony but also my life. Always remember First Samuel 1:22: "Obedience is better than sacrifice."

So I know you are wondering what I did to calm my holiday heartburn! God sent me on a shopping spree, and I had the most wonderful time! What I did not tell you was that I was starting a new job at the beginning of the year and was in need of a few new things. Well, as God would have it, my favorite store had a wonderful sale, and God provided me with some extra money. So I went shopping. It was a great day, and at the end of the day, I had a pair of new pajamas, my favorite food, and my expensive sparkling cider. I watched some wonderful Hallmark movies, and at 11:30 p.m., I was on my knees praying and praising God for his protection, provision, and love. I also had the opportunity to spend some time talking on the phone to a wonderful friend, so I was not alone after all.

My holiday heartburn became an awesome holiday celebration—God's way!

Woman to Woman

Yes, my holiday heartburn could have been a lot worse. I am reminded of First Peter 5:8, which warns, "Be sober, be vigilant; because your adversary the devil, as a roaring lion, walketh about, seeking whom he may devour." God needs us to be sober in our thinking, vigilant in our hearts, and obedient to his prompting. I believe it is this type of relationship with God that will keep us safe from hurt, harm, and danger while dealing with our holiday heartburn.

I believe that desiring to be married is as natural as breathing. I also believe that God knows the perfect time and person to whom you are to be married. Sometimes, the holidays make waiting that much harder, but you still must wait if and only if you truly want God's best for your life.

Being Honest with God

1. Which holidays are your holiday heartburn, and why?

   _____

   _____

   _____

   _____

2. In the past, how have you spent those holidays?

   _____

   _____

   _____

   _____

3. What short-term and long-term consequences did those decisions create (if any)?

_____

_____

_____

_____

4. What is your holiday celebration plan for the future?

_____

_____

_____

_____

Journaling with God

9

On Lockdown

Be still and know that I am God.

—Psalms 46:10

What do you do when God makes you invisible to the opposite sex? Do you praise Him? Are you angry with Him? Are you obedient and follow His plans for your life even when you do not understand His plans or want them?

Lockdown is a form of protection (mainly from yourself) because God has a very special plan for your life. It is a shield of protection from the enemy. Before you start shouting how men are the enemy, I am not talking about men. I am talking about that thing that goes wherever you go. I am talking about your flesh! We oftentimes do not have the mental and physical capacity or strength to say no. Therefore, God places His supernatural plan of protection around us, which I call God's lockdown system.

Let me share with you what God's lockdown looks like. It looks like you can't get a date! No matter how pretty, intelligent, spiritual, kindhearted, sweet, and understanding you are, men just do not seem to pay any attention to you. They will talk to you and even consider you their little sister or big sister, but not their girlfriend. Romantically speaking, you are invisible to them. Why? God has you on lockdown, and only He possesses the key to freedom.

You know you are on lockdown when your ex-boyfriends will not even call to ask you out. They may even go so far as to tell you that they made a mistake by breaking up with you, but they have since moved on and considered you a friend. When you are longing for love and marriage, the last thing you want is to be somebody's friend!

You are suddenly invisible to the opposite sex. Don't worry. It is not forever, but it can last for a while. This lockdown is done for a purpose. God has a special assignment for you, and if He would allow your flesh to get loose, you would ruin what God has for you and the people He needs you to reach in ministry.

Noah was chosen to build the Ark, just as Moses had to be the one to lead the children of Israel out of bondage. There is a plan and purpose for your life, and at this time in your life, a man cannot be involved. Thus, God has made you His for a specific purpose. The question is will you accept the assignment God has for you, or will you fight God's plan because you cannot have what you want right now?

Whether you realize it or not, lockdown is truly a place of protection in your life; it is also a place of refuge. Many times in our lockdown status, we find that God desires to be the main person in our life. First Corinthians 11:2 says, "For I am jealous over you with godly jealousy: for I have espoused you to one husband, that I may present [you as] a chaste virgin to Christ."

Think about the last time you were in a relationship with someone. Did God remain first in your life? What compromises did you make in your relationship with God in order to keep your relationship with the man in your life going? Do you believe Psalm 84:11, "For the Lord God is a sun and a shield: the Lord will give grace and glory: no good thing will he withhold from them that walk uprightly?"

With that being said, if dating or having a husband at this time is a good thing, then would not God provide it for you? That is the bottom line. He will not withhold any good thing from you. There are lessons to be learned during your lockdown that cannot and will not be learned while dating. God wants your full attention for whatever reason He has chosen. If you are looking for a reason, God does not owe you or anyone else an answer as to why He chooses to direct our lives in a certain manner. Remember Job, he never got an answer for the test, trial and temporary assignment God has him on. However, the Bible does say his end was better than his beginning. Now that is something we can hold on to.

I'm reminded of this old hymn that says, "Have thine own way, Lord have thine own way! Thou art the Potter, I am the clay. Mold me and make me after Thy will, while I am waiting, yielded and still." I love this verse. It says mold me and make me after Thy will. When you are on lockdown mode, what do you think God is doing? He is molding every area of your life, while you are waiting, yielding, and being still. It is pretty hard to mold someone if they are moving all over the place, but He can definitely mold you if He has you still. What better way to know that you are in God's will when you are perfectly still, waiting on Him to make each and every move regarding your life?

Be careful and do not think of this time of lockdown as disciplinary action from God because it is not. Oftentimes, we see everyone else in relationships: our sisters, girlfriends, cousins, and mothers. Other women around us are dating and getting married, and we cannot even get a date to the weddings. Being on lockdown means you will attend many functions alone. Once you find peace in the lockdown season of your life, attending events and functions will not be as difficult.

The challenge with living on lockdown is finding contentment. Of course, you will not find God's peace in this season as long as your eyes are on someone else's life (see Hebrews 4:11). Women are known for longing for what they do not have. We often miss the blessings God has for us in various seasons of our lives because we are too busy drooling after some other woman's life of perceived comfort and enjoyment.

We want her body type, her hairstyle, her house, her husband, and her children. We even have the nerve to be envious of her relationship with God (see Hebrews 13:5). Yes, this scripture is well-known, but we only quote the latter half, which says "God will never leave us nor forsake us." What about the first part that says stop coveting and be content with your life right now? If we would apply this simple scripture to our lives, being on lockdown by God would not be so difficult.

It is like fasting. If all you ever think about during the fast is food, then you will never be able to hear God or even complete the fast. Isaiah 26:3 encourages that "Thou wilt keep him in perfect peace, whose mind is stayed on thee: because he trusted in thee." When your mind is stayed on Christ, having the peace of God is not difficult. In actuality, it is very hard not to have peace when your mind is on Christ.

This lockdown season will be very instrumental to your growth if you utilize this time God has given you wisely. Your prayer life will be strengthened, your knowledge of God's Word will expand, and your relationship with God will deepen. By learning who God is and what He desires for you, your life will be enriched. God has separated you for such a time as this just for Him. You may not always see it as a blessing, but how you come out on the other side will define who you are as a godly woman for the rest of your life.

How long will you be on lockdown? I do not know, but God does. You will be on lockdown as long as He needs you to be. Each woman's lockdown season is different because God has something different for each woman. One woman may experience lockdown for six months while another's will last six years. However long God wants to spend time with you, I would advise that you take full advantage of it.

In case you did not like that answer, 1 Timothy 6:6 says, "But godliness with contentment is great gain." This has everything to do with our attitude. A godly attitude coupled with contentment always sows fruit that God can use. Will your initial response be one of contentment? I doubt it; however, once you realize God is doing something special in your life, your attitude should be gracious so that other women can benefit from your experiences.

The great gain will be what lessons and experiences you bring at the end of your lockdown season. I am sure these lessons will be ones you can use in marriage, work, parenthood, ministry, and any other of life's seasons God has for you. Believe me when I say that I know how difficult this time can be, but it does not have to be. You will be able to build wonderful relationships during this season, and those relationships will help strengthen you through this time. For me, it has been these strong sisters of faith that have reminded me of God's grace and mercy in my lockdown season. Have I liked it? No, but oh how I have learned to appreciate my life and my alone time with God!

In case you still want to know how long, the answer is that the duration is different for each woman, depending on the plan He has for your life. God has equipped each of us with our own gifts. He also has a different plan for each of our lives. Only God Himself knows how long it will take to perfect His plan and His gifts in our lives. Some of us are more disobedient than others. For those women who love men to the point that they lose their minds and sense of reality, it may take God some time to get your full attention.

Personally Speaking

God has had me on lockdown for a long time. When it started, I was a single mom and my first ministry was my children. I have to admit that I would not have the relationship I have with my children or in ministry if God had not locked down me and my flesh. I am grateful because I realize that there was so much I needed to learn, so much I needed to let go of in my life, and so many things I needed to get right in my heart.

I needed God to lock me down. You see I thought my life was about me, how cute and how sexy I was. In that state of mind, God was not important and neither was His Word. As if that was not enough, my children were second to my needs. However, God made it plain He wanted to be in control of my life. Once I embraced His plans for my life, I stopped trying to get the attention of men. My true heart's desire was to be a godly woman and mother. I wanted to be what God wanted me to be, even if it meant being a great single mom and a servant of the Lord Jesus Christ. Whatever He wanted me to be, I became content.

I am still not married, and I am satisfied in my season of singleness. I do not dread being on lockdown as much anymore because I know God has a wonderful plan for my life. It may or may not include a husband. Regardless of His ultimate plan, I am confident of this very thing—it is going to be fun, exciting and full of His grace, mercy, and unconditional love for my family and me.

I also had something else to learn while being on lockdown by God. It meant He wanted to be personally responsible for every need of my family. It is awesome to know that He loves me so much that he became personally responsible for my every need as well as my family's need in this season of lockdown. He gave me the vision to start a Ministry for Single Moms, as well as gave me a gift to write books such as the one you hold in your hands. I realize I could never have accomplished these things had God not placed me on lockdown to get my full attention. I'm not saying he couldn't do these things if I were married, it just wouldn't have been as easy, at least not for me, if He had not placed me on lockdown and made me invisible to men. I praise Him for this special time in my life. It allowed me to be totally committed to and dependent on Him for everything in my and my children's lives.

Although this was a very scary time in my life as I depended on God to fulfill my every financial, emotional, physical, and spiritual need, I knew He would carry me when I was weak. He would humble me when pride entered my heart. He would lead and guide my steps in every decision I made. I understood the position of a husband in the family and how he is responsible for all of his family's needs. However, God had chosen to be my husband and the Father to my children, and I let Him. Reflecting over my years of lockdown, I do not regret one second, minute, or hour of the time I have spent with God.

I have to admit that I have not taken total advantage of His time with me, I am still learning. I am learning that time waits for no one, and when God talks, listen and obey whatever He instructs you to do. When He gives me a Saturday that's free, I need to take that time to read His Word, spend time in prayer thanking and beseeching Him on behalf of my family, friends, and myself instead of watching television or playing on Facebook as I often do. I have to stay in His Word for protection from my very flesh.

Woman to Woman

If you have found yourself on lockdown (regardless of how long), do not be mad, angry, or frustrated that you cannot get a date or even catch a man's attention. Get happy, place yourself in the arms of Jesus, and say it is well with my soul. God has a special plan for you, and He needs your full attention in order to perfect His plan in you.

Do as Samuel did in 1st Samuel 3. He heard someone calling him, and he thought it was Eli, but it was the Lord. When Eli realized what was going on, he told Samuel that when he heard the voice call him again, to do the following: "Go, lie down and it shall be if He call thee that thou shalt say 'Speak Lord; for thy servant heareth.' So Samuel went and lay down in his place" (1 Samuel 3:9).

What is my point? If you know God has you on lockdown, tell Him, "Speak Lord, for thy servant heareth you, and I will obey you Lord. Have your way *in* my life and *with* my life Lord. Mold me and shape me so that I can be a vessel fit for the Master's use."

You will not regret this very special time God has set aside in your life. This is His time to teach you His Word, give you His wisdom, and shower you with His unconditional love and protection.

Being Honest with God

1. How long have you been on lockdown?

   _____

   _____

   _____

   _____

2. In what ways have you tried to escape lockdown (e.g., text, e-mail, Skype, etc.)?

   _____

   _____

   _____

   _____

3. What has God revealed to you about His plans for you during your season of lockdown?

_____

_____

_____

_____

4. How will you spend your time of lockdown from now on?

_____

_____

_____

_____

Journaling with God

10

RED FLAGS MEAN STOP!

*There hath no temptation taken you but such as is
common to man: but God is faithful, who will not
suffer you to be tempted above that you are able; but
will with the temptation also make a way to escape,
that ye may able to bear it.*

—1 Corinthians 10:13

I have been in several relationships, and in all of them, I experienced physical, emotional, and spiritual abuse. Those were very difficult times in my life. However, I take full responsibility for them. The men were either not Christians at the time or babes in Christ and carnal at best. Although I was not as spiritually mature as I am now, I knew better but I wanted my way. I just had to get married, and that is what I did twice. I should have never married either man to begin with. Both marriages ended in divorce. I did what I wanted to do and could have lost my life. I was warned both times not to marry either man, but I justified my actions by painting a picture of them that I knew in my heart was a lie. I wanted to be married at any cost and paid dearly for my disobedience.

Marriage should enhance our lives, not diminish it. You will have difficult times, but 90 percent of your marriage should not be filled with arguing, screaming, and fighting. That was what both marriages consisted of, including infidelity. However, in my time with the Lord, I have found out that I don't need a man to be my anything if he can't enhance my everything.

Has God given you any signs regarding the person you are dating? I am asking because God will not allow you to be deceived. There will be red flags and usually more than one. Will you know them when you see them? Our problem as women is that we believe we can change the men in our lives. We think we will make the difference in his life, when in reality God is the only one who can do that. I am here to tell you that if God cannot change a man, then why do you think you can? God may have allowed you to be in this person's life to enlighten him about Christ but not to marry him. This is the very reason why I believe that women should not counsel men. Due to our emotional state, we have the ability to get confused and are ready to head to the altar to marry, when in reality we should have just gone to the altar for prayer.

We sometimes miss the red flags because we ignore them, not because we do not see them. Abuse comes in many forms, from verbal to physical and all those in between.

Twice I married men I hardly knew. At the end of the day, I wanted to be married and wanted that picture-perfect family. I had two children and wanted a husband for me and a father for my children to complete my life. The truth of the matter is that God did not need my help in this area. If I had just been obedient and still, I would have noticed that God was taking good care of me and my children. I did not need a husband.

This little disobedient act could have also cost me my children because they truly did not like either man. If you are a single mom, please protect your children by not marrying the wrong man. I also want to add that children are intuitive. Listen to them and watch how they respond to this man in your life; they don't usually dislike adults for no reason. To emphasize my point, I am going to make a statement that was made to me after my second divorce. A statement that I thought I would never make. Here it is: *if you are a single mom, I would strongly advise that you not marry until your children are grown and have left the home.* They deserve to have all of you to themselves. When children are five years and older, and you add a husband to the family, usually it causes problems. No matter how wonderful the man is, there are many adjustments that will have to be made. One of those adjustments will be the time you spend with your children versus the time you spend getting to know and building your relationship with your new husband.

I remember when one of my spiritual mothers told me I should wait until my children were out of the house before

I marry again. I looked at her as if she had lost her mind. She had a husband waiting for her at home, and she wanted me to wait! I can tell you right now that I had no intentions of waiting, but I am so glad God changed my heart and my mind regarding this situation. This is where I can see God's amazing grace all over my life, and this is when I was placed on lockdown. No one saw me in a romantic way, and if they did, they certainly did not say anything to me. It is as if God made me invisible to the opposite sex. This was for my protection, and to this day I'm still grateful. I truly would not have the close-knit and wonderful relationship I have with my daughter and son had I brought yet another man into their lives, trying to provide them a father. In actuality they already had everything they needed, which was a mother who loved them and a heavenly Father who loved them more than me and would provide for and protect them.

Blatant Red Flags

Do you know what the acronym for STOP is? Well, let me share it with you: S-surveillance, T-threat, O-obstacle, and P-proceed. God desires us to be wise; "Behold I send you forth as sheep in the midst of wolves: be ye therefore wise as serpents, and harmless as doves" (Matthew 10:16). Ladies, using the STOP acronym will assist in providing us with answers that are not obvious. Please do your homework. I used to be an identity theft investigator, so I am very good at finding out things. Therefore, by all means use the stop method to investigate this man, his friends, and family.

What type of man are you really getting ready to marry? Do you even know the type of man he truly is when no one is watching? So many women are in their graves because they did not take the time to get to know the men they loved and who claimed to love them. Then, there are those who knew the truth but believed he would change in time, thereby deceiving themselves into believing a lie, a lie that killed them and/or their children.

Learn to look for the signs of even subtle red flags. They may look pink instead of red. Err on the side of caution. They can be anything, from calling you every five minutes when you are not in his sight to accusations of indecent behavior when you do not answer his calls or return his calls within his time frame. They can also include his having temper tantrums when he does not get his way. Many times, temper tantrums can escalate into more verbally and physically aggressive behavior, like getting in your face, grabbing you, or cursing you. Ladies, anytime a man allows himself to get so angry that he gets in your face to make you think he will hit you, he will hit you eventually. Hitting may ultimately lead to someone's death, and it may be yours or your children's. If you are in such a relationship, get out now and seek help today!

I also must add that if you are the insecure abuser, then he needs to say good-bye to you, and you need to seek help for anger management as well as potential unresolved issues in your life that are now manifesting themselves in violent behavior.

Ephesians 5:28–29 states, "So ought men to love their wives as their own bodies. He that loveth his wife loveth himself. For no man ever yet hated his own flesh; but nourisheth and cherisheth it, even as the Lord the church." This scripture clearly tells you that there should not be any form of abuse in a relationship. You cannot love someone and hurt them at the same time. If a man says "I love you" and hits you or has jealous urges, he is lying. If you do and say the same thing to him, you are lying.

Another red flag is in the form of name-calling and belittling, which are also signs of verbal and/or mental abuse. Many times, women will justify his verbal actions by saying, "He doesn't hit me. He just gets mad and says things he doesn't really mean." Ladies, if he did not mean them, he would not have said them. Therefore, he means them. He just may not have meant to say them when he did. Just like a man does not hit a woman he truly loves, so he will not verbally hurt her either.

Back in the day, do you remember the saying, "Sticks and stones may break my bones, but words will never hurt me?" Well, that is also a lie. Words do hurt and are often used to tear people down. When spoken with the right amount of venom, they can cut deeper than physical scars and last long after the scars have faded or even disappeared. Unkind, demeaning, and hateful words should not be ignored. Unfortunately, we live in times now where it is acceptable in and out of the church to curse and call people everything but the name on their birth certificates. If your boyfriend or fiancé grew up in an environment where that behavior was the norm, then it is time to educate him on how you will and will not be addressed. If he disregards your wishes and continues with this behavior, you must know that things will only get worse if you choose to marry him.

Keep in mind that this only works if you are not cursing him and disrespecting him. If you do not treat him that way, why would you allow him treat you with less respect than you provide him? Let's think about this for a moment. Picture the men in your life who honor you, love you, and value you. It can be your father, grandfather, brother, uncle, friend, or even your pastor. Have any of these men who honor, love, and value you ever called you stupid, dumb, ugly, fat, ignorant, or worthless? No, they have not and neither should anyone else! Your heavenly Father doesn't call you bad names, and you know you've made decisions that were not pleasing to him yet he still refers to you as his daughter.

Red flags are warnings. Do not ignore them. Recognize them, address them, pray about them, and obey God in how He tells you to deal with them. Your decision to obey God's direction will determine the difference between a great healthy relationship and a divorce and have an impact on the life of your children. We all get angry. People disappoint us, and we disappoint them—we're human. Ephesians 4:26 warns, "Be angry but sin not." How we handle those difficult and trying times indicates our character as well as our spiritual maturity. It is easy to say what we will and will not do until we are actually in a situation that requires us to think before we respond. This is something we should require of ourselves and the one we hope to marry.

James 1:19 warns, "Wherefore, my beloved brethren, let every man be swift to hear, slow to speak, slow to wrath." This scripture should be a quality we require in any man we date and believe God would have us to marry. Ignoring this principle can have costly consequences.

Potential Red Flags

(Incorporate the STOP system: Surveillance, Threat, Obstacle and Proceed)

Potential red flags could be his relationship with his mother or father, ungodly habits, family addictions, and infidelity in previous relationships. Old baggage or unresolved issues from his childhood may be a red flag, such as what type of relationship did or does he have with his mother? Is it a relationship of love, respect, and reverence? Was he raised with both parents in the home, or by his mother, father, or another relative such as grandmother, aunt, uncle, cousin, or even someone outside of his biological family? I ask because many times the way a man treats his mother can be indicative of how he'll treat his girlfriend or wife. From Exodus to Ephesians, ten times the Bible says to honor thy mother and father. However, God didn't place a codicil in his word that says if they didn't raise you or if they aren't perfect parents, you don't have to be. Whatever issues he has with his parents, if forgiveness has not been implemented in his life, this should be a red flag.

Communication in any relationship is so very important especially when the word *marriage* is being discussed. This is where you need to know things such as a family history of drug abuse of any kind. What type of relationship did his mom and dad have? Was he subjected to domestic violence in the home, whether with Mom and Dad or with a stepparent (i.e., stepmom or stepdad)? Was he a victim of domestic violence or abuse of any kind? These are issues that many times just never come up, and I don't know why. If you are going to enter into a covenant with someone, why wouldn't you want to know these things? Certainly not knowing could mean the difference between life and death to you and or your children if you are a single mom.

Another issue women will skirt around is mental illness. Is there a history of mental illness of any kind in his family? The list is just too vast for me to mention, but you need to know this is not just a safety issue but, if you are going to have children with this man, this could be passed on to your children. Ladies, do your homework! Marriage is a lifelong commitment, and it is just too important to skate around issues that could cause you an insurmountable amount of pain in your life and the life of your children not to mention this could spill over to other relatives. I know you've heard of a spouse killing his wife, children, her mother and father, and sometimes friends have even been harmed by an out-of-control husband. Do your homework before you bring a person that has unresolved issues into your life.

Understand I'm not saying that if this man has a history of these things in his life, the relationship is automatically over. I'm saying know who and what you are dealing with before you commit to a relationship with someone you don't know. In the beginning of the book, I said women are excited about the wedding, men are excited about the honeymoon, and no one is discussing the marriage, which is what you will live for the rest of your life. That is why this phrase will be mentioned many times throughout this book because it is important, and I want you to live a life of happiness. Ever see the movie *Enough* with Jennifer Lopez? If you haven't, then go out today and rent that movie. It is a powerful story of not knowing someone before you marry them. These are scary times, and again I use Gods warning in 1st Peter 5:8, "Be sober, be vigilant; because your adversary the devil, as a roaring lion, walketh about, seeking whom he may devour." Think about the word devour; what does a lion do to his prey? He kills it, there is literally nothing left of his prey. This is the mindset of the enemy regarding Christians. Do you not think the devil can use marriage as a tool to destroy you? Do you think that the sanctity of marriage means anything to the deceiver of the world? Well, let me tell you it doesn't mean a thing to him. Life as we know it means nothing to him; he is after your very soul and the soul of your children, and if he can get them by destroying marriage, which is what God ordained, then he'll do it. Again, ladies, be wise on matters of the heart because it can be a life-and-death issue.

Although the subjects I am about to address are not themselves a red flag, I do believe they have the potential to be one. Discuss these subjects prior to getting married or even engaged because they are issues that will come up in your marriage.

Discipline

When you are in the midst of your conversations, and you are talking about having children, please discuss how and who will discipline the children. The Bible is candid about spanking children in such scriptures as Proverbs 13:24, Proverbs 23:13–14, and Proverbs 19:18.

Find out what your future husband believes about this subject. You all need to be on one accord on this because children have the potential to play one parent against the other, and if you've already discussed this during premarital counseling, you can have a united front. Let me share with you my experience with this. My son's father and I were never married and when that relationship ended, we both agreed that we wanted what was right for our son.

Discipline was something we both grew up with and on which we both agreed, so if my son was on punishment at my house and went to spend the weekend with his dad, his punishment followed him there; meaning, if I said no television for a week when he went to his dad's house, he couldn't watch television over there either. Do you know how that would infuriate our son? But we didn't care. We wanted him first to know that we loved him enough to get past whatever differences we had in our relationship. If my son called his dad to complain about something I did, his dad would promptly say, "Let me talk to your Mom." He never took my son's word over mine, and I didn't do it to him. We worked together to make sure my son knew you can't play us against each other. So having a united front will be important. "Can two walk together, except they be agreed?" (Amos 3:3).

Our Home?

Here is another consideration—where will you live? If you both have your own places, then a decision, no doubt, will have to be made. This can be complicated, but it doesn't have to be. There is nothing wrong with compromise and this should be a simple decision. It may be simply whose living quarters are larger, or you also may consider distance as far as your jobs are concerned. Some people have no problem with commuting, but I do. I don't like to drive; therefore, I would like to live close to my job. Again, compromise would still be necessary, no doubt, but if you fireproof this with a discussion ahead of time, this won't cause an unnecessary problem.

Where to Live

Another subject you'll want to agree on is whether you will live in the suburbs or in the inner city. If you both grew up in the same state, will you stay close to family, or will you be willing to move to another state if your husband is offered a better job opportunity? Or if you are offered a better opportunity, will he be willing to relocate? These issues may seem minute now, but they will be most important in your future.

Discuss them openly, honestly, and candidly because if you don't, they will come up again, and one or both of you will say, "If I'd known this, I might not have married you." Start now placing protective barriers around your marriage so as not to let the enemy slip in and destroy what God has put together. You can do that simply by honestly communicating your feelings and thoughts about the hard issues. I know many times women won't communicate their true feelings as they don't want to miss out on the opportunity of marriage.

If you do that, you could end up married to the wrong person, and I can tell you there is something worse than not being married: being married to someone who doesn't love you, your God, or your children (if you happen to be a single mom). It is a horrible existence. Read what love is and what it isn't in 1st Corinthians 13, and if you have questions after you read it, talk with your pastor. I'm telling you this book was written to protect you, not to scare you out of wanting to be married but to make you aware of what marriage really is and is not. Marriage is not just about sex—yes, that is part of it but a small part—and I've mentioned that previously, but I want you to get it. I really do. I want you, ladies, to know I wrote this book because God loves you so very much. He wants you to operate out of a spirit of truth, wisdom, knowledge, and understanding. "Wisdom is the principal thing; therefore get wisdom: and with all thy getting get understanding" (Proverbs 4:7).

Children from Prior Relationships

When dating and desiring to marry a man with children from a previous relationship, there are additional red flags for which you must be alert. This situation can be difficult, and it can cause a great deal of pain for everyone involved if you do not seek and receive godly counsel and God's guidance. You have to realize that a man with children from a previous relationship has a dual relationship with his children's mother. First, you have the romantic relationship between them as a man and woman. How was the door closed to that relationship? Who closed it? If he did not close it or fought to keep it open, then he may not be ready to enter into the lifelong commitment of marriage, no matter how many times he says "I love you."

The second aspect of their relationship is the one of father and mother: this is the relationship that lasts forever. Their child will always keep them connected throughout that child's life. Any attempt on your part to place yourself as priority over his relationship with his child will jeopardize your chances of being in his life at all, especially if the child is young. You will need to ask the hard questions: Whose idea was it to have a baby? What's your relationship with the mother? How's your relationship with his child(ren)? How do you fit in his life with his child(ren)?

Please know that if you are going to be woman enough to ask these questions, you better be woman enough to receive the answers he gives you. Finally, you have to be woman enough to answer those same questions when he asks you. If you cannot be honest with him regarding your feelings for the father of your children, that door is not closed, and you are not ready to get married.

Believe me when I say that it takes a lot to be married when it is just the two of you. Blended families require even more work because you are blending multiple families. There are so many dynamics to consider when parents marry with children from other relationships. I am not saying that it cannot work. I just want you to think about the short-term and long-term impact before you commit yourself and your children to a situation that can be equally as painful as the one you just left. By the way, if he has more than one child by more than one woman, that is a big red flag!

Church Home

Another topic you might want to consider discussing is what church your family will attend. If the Bible is your foundation for the way you live your life, and you have accepted Jesus as your personal Lord and Savior, then church should be a normal part of your life. Hebrews 10:25 explains why we should attend church.

Whose church will you attend once you are married is a decision that should be made before the marriage actually takes place. Actually, this discussion should be known before you get too serious. Now I know many would say the woman should leave her church; I don't think that necessarily is the truth. I believe it should be based on ministry involvement. No doubt if you are marrying a minister, pastor, or a man who is in leadership in his church you may have to leave your church. I know you may be saying, what about my ministry? I hear you loud and clear. That is why fireproofing your relationship now will make a big difference in your future. If you are in leadership at your church, you may have to step down if your potential husband is in leadership at his church, remembering that you are in the position of being a help meet.

Woman to Woman

The Word of God makes the true definition of love so plain. In the Bible, God refers to love as charity, which is an action word (not a feeling word). First Corinthians 13:4–8 describes very clearly what love is and is not:

> Charity suffereth long, [and] is kind; charity envieth not; charity vaunteth not itself, is not puffed up, Doth not behave itself unseemly, seeketh not her own, is not easily provoked, thinketh no evil; Rejoiceth not in iniquity, but rejoiceth in the truth; Beareth all things, believeth all things, hopeth all things, endureth all things. Charity never faileth: but whether [there be] prophecies, they shall fail; whether [there be] tongues, they shall cease; whether [there be] knowledge, it shall vanish away. (King James Version)

God is very clear about His definition of love. Heed to these words of wisdom. Let them guide you on how you should be treated, not only as a potential help meet but also as his sister in Christ. We must be careful with this concept of dating because we often forget that God does not want us to be harmed physically, spiritually, or emotionally. However, because of our fear of loneliness, we often settle for anyone who looks our way without ever discerning the motives of his heart. In the process, we allow men to tear down what God is building up.

Being Honest with God

1. What is your true fear?

_____

_____

_____

_____

2. Are you afraid Gods plan is different than your plan for your life?

_____

_____

_____

_____

5. _____?

6. _____?

Journaling with God

11

CHOOSE ME!

*And ye are complete in him, which is the
head of all principality and power.*

—Colossians 2:10

THE STATEMENT "CHOOSE me" is a desperate plea for love. Since God's love is unconditional and everlasting, you do not have to beg for it. Therefore, if you find yourself begging for a man to choose you, you have gone outside the protection of your heavenly Father. Requesting someone to choose you means that you have decided to take things into your own hands in order to take the quickest route to the altar. Let me ask you this: Who chose this man to be your husband? Did God choose him, or did you? Did your family choose him even though their humanity makes them flawed at best, leaving you prey to the enemy, possibly for the rest of your life? The "choose me" attitude will always make you settle for a lot less than what God wants and desires for you to have in your life.

Marriages based upon your choice or even your fiancé's choice can turn out to be many times a marriage of bondage, which is not what God intended marriage to represent. If you truly desire to have the happily-ever-after marriage, then God must choose for you. As you know, this will require you to stay in your place as a godly woman who trusts God's choice in God's time. Submitting to God's will means you will have to change your thinking about letting someone choose you. If you are manipulating situations in order to get a man to notice you or choose you as his wife (like getting pregnant on purpose, or having sex outside of marriage), you are in control, not God.

First John 4:19 says that we love him because He first loved us. We understand this scripture so clearly for all the things Jesus went through to prove his love for us. Then we read Romans 5:8, "But God commendeth his love toward us, in that, while we were yet sinners, Christ died for us." We are so busy looking for love in all the wrong places we forget the incredible love story God wrote for us, a story that reminds us that God chose to save us. God chose to use us as His earthly vessels in order that we may draw others to Him.

Being chosen by God means you are part of the royal family. God is the King of Kings and Lord of Lords (see 1 Peter 2:9). He owns a vast kingdom that has no ending. His power has no boundaries, and His resources are limitless. He is omniscient (all-knowing), omnipotent (all-powerful) (see

Revelations 19:6), and omnipresent (everywhere all the time). When you truly begin to believe that God is all of these things and more, you will not beg someone to choose you.

Choose me is an attitude that we should only have toward God. Lord, choose me to serve you. Choose me to send. Choose me to be a voice to those who do not know you. Choose me to be a godly help meet to the husband you have chosen for me in your time. We can often feel we have been overlooked by the men in our churches and our communities; therefore, we feel the need to plead our case to them as to why we should be their wife. Unfortunately, because men do not think like women, they mistake our choose me attitude for something totally different that usually has nothing to do with marriage. Because we have been so candid about our feelings and our methods, men think we will settle for anything, including compromising our desire to be a help meet and settling on being a girlfriend, bed partner, or simply a friend with benefits. Due to our fear of never getting married, we will allow this type of degrading behavior to become our destiny. It is true that many physical relationships lead to marriage for various reasons, but you will never know if he married you for the woman you are in Christ or for how you served him in the bedroom.

Another way of having a man choose you is to ask family and friends to introduce you to someone. You are still not waiting on God as I mentioned in chapter 3, "Why Wait on God?" As long as you are walking around in the choose me mode, God has no reason to choose for you. We must lose this desperate attitude. How? Stop overdressing for events. Stop trying to be the loudest or funniest as a means to draw your targeted suitor's attention toward you. If God wants to get his attention for you, He is very capable of doing so and does not need your help.

You may be more passive with your methods, so you do not say it with your voice, but you say it with your eyes when the gift you receive is not the engagement ring you have been wanting. You say it in your silence when you find out that he has betrayed you, but you do not know how you can go on without him. You show it when you compromise your beliefs; you know he does not serve God but maybe one day he will. You say "choose me" every time you call him first when he makes no effort to call you for days. With each come hither glance and smile, you slip farther and farther away from your position in the Kingdom of God. Each choose me act reveals to the world and God that you have forgotten that your Father is a King, thereby making you His princess. Therefore, you do not need to beg anyone to choose you.

Do you remember when I previously talked about having a meek and gentle spirit that is of great price in the sight of God? If so, don't you think you need to get somewhere, sit down and get quiet? "Be still and know that I am God" (Psalms 46:10). Get quiet and see Him show you favor with someone you thought would never look your way. Get quiet and rest in God's arms when you are weary and scared that you will be single for the rest of your life. Get quiet and trust that God has His very best waiting for you, but He is waiting for you to stop choosing.

Ladies, we are so busy choosing our husbands that we forget that if God could be born of a virgin, part the Red Sea, feed His children manna from heaven, protect David from Saul, feed five thousand with two fish and five loaves of bread with leftovers, calm the angry waters, spare Jonah to save the people of Ninevah, give water from a rock, walk on water, die on the cross, and rise again on the third day, don't you think He can choose and preserve a husband for you? Well, He can. The question is will you move out of His way and watch Him prepare an amazing journey of love, marriage, and happiness for you?

Woman to Woman

"Choose ye this day whom you will serve!" (Joshua 24:15). Will you serve the living God with your obedience of praise and thanksgiving, choosing to trust Him to act on your behalf in choosing a husband for you? He still answers knee mails (prayer).

Being Honest with God

1. _____?

   _____

   _____

   _____

   _____

2. _____?

   _____

   _____

   _____

   _____

3. _____?

_____

_____

_____

_____

4. _____?

_____

_____

_____

_____

Journaling with God

12

Expectations

My soul, wait thou only upon God;
for my expectation [is] from him.

—Psalms 62:5

God has some expectations of us. He expects us to love Him with our whole hearts, souls, minds, and bodies according to Deuteronomy 6:5. God expects us to obey Him (Isaiah 18–20). He expects us to pray (Luke 11:2) and to forgive (Luke 11:4). Since these are things that God expects of us, they are things we should also expect of ourselves.

In addition to God having expectations of people, society has certain expectations as well. If you have a job, the expectation is that you will go to work every day, be on time, and work your shift. In turn, you have an expectation of receiving a paycheck, right? Of course you do. Most people do not work for free.

If you have children, you are expected to take care of them, not your parents, not your grandparents, not society, but you. Regardless of your age, race, color, ethnicity, creed, or gender, there are expectations for your life. Some of them are realistic; others are not. We as women have expectations for ourselves. Again, some are realistic and some are not. Some are cultural. Some have been created by society's view of women.

Sometimes, we base our expectations on the lives of our girlfriends. For instance, if her boyfriend opens doors and does other nice things for her, we will then begin to expect that same behavior from the men in our lives. Ladies, for the record, no man wants to be compared to another man even if he is not an ex-boyfriend, just like you do not want someone basing their expectations of you on another person. Whether it is his mother's sweet potato pie recipe or his cousin's new hairdo, we do not take kindly to being expected to act a certain way or to fulfill certain duties because of what someone else is doing in his life.

Women have lots of expectations of men when they are dating. The more exclusive the relationship, the more expectations we have. However, we must understand they are not our husbands; therefore, some of our expectations of these men are beyond the boundaries of their relationship with us as their girlfriend, such as paying our bills, helping us pay our bills, doing household chores at our houses, and babysitting our children when he is not their father. The reverse is also true. He should not have any expectations of you cooking his dinner, having sex, washing and ironing his clothes, or buying his groceries. Why? You are not his wife, and he is not your husband! Men and women alike get so caught up in their dating relationship that they forget to set healthy boundaries. "All things are lawful for me, but all things are not expedient: all things are lawful for me, but all things edify not" (1Corinthians 10:23).

The Word of God has all the answers to all of life's situations and circumstances. It is clear that while you have the expectations of the man in your life to cut your lawn, wash your car, and help you pay your bills, according to 1st Corinthians 10:23, should he be doing those things? Remember, he is not your husband and you are not his wife. Even referring to him as your husband when you have yet to be married as required by law is crossing the line. What if you do not marry him? Are you going to refer to your next boyfriend as your husband? If so, the term will not mean anything to you once you have a legal husband. It also will not mean as much to him once he realizes that every man you dated was given the title and benefits which he had not earned (by marrying you). Marriage is too special for us to give the title away to anyone and everyone we date.

You know we are part of the body of Christ, and God refers to us as His sheep, His children. We are also called Christians, which means little Christ. Now how preposterous would it be for a person who does not believe in Christ and was not a born-gain Christian to start referring to him/herself as a Christian? You would think they were silly, wouldn't you? Well, it is the same principle. Why would you honor any man with the title of being your husband when they have not married you? You are placing the cart before the horse, and you are setting yourself up for heartbreak. As a final note, if he dies while you are dating, having given him the title of husband without a valid marriage does not entitle you to anything he owns.

Healthy Expectations

Now that we have talked about the expectations we should not have, what are some expectations that we should have for ourselves, the men we are dating, or the men we hope to marry? I am glad you asked. While some women have unrealistic expectations, others have no expectations at all and will accept anything that looks in their direction. That is just as wrong.

Ladies, we must have some expectations, and they must align with God's Word. The first expectation that comes to mind is that he must be a born-again Christian, according to 2nd Corinthians 6:14. Guess what? You should be too! I believe being equally yoked goes far beyond just him being a Christian. I believe it also refers to your denominations as well. Although you can marry someone of another denomination, that denomination's teachings and beliefs can cause huge problems even if he is a Christian and loves the Lord.

Amos 3:3 asks, "Can two walk together, except they be agreed?" I will let you answer that question. Nevertheless, I must remind you of your place as a help meet according to

1st Corinthians 11:3, which explains, "But I would have you know, that the head of every man is Christ; and the head of the woman is the man; and the head of Christ is God." Once we marry, we become our husband's help meet. We are to help him meets his needs, his responsibilities, and his destiny in Christ. While we are doing that naturally, he will be doing the same for us. If Christ is the head of every man, and man is the head of the woman, don't you want your husband serving God according to the same teachings and beliefs that shaped your relationship with God?

Now that we have established the importance of being equally yoked on more than just the level of being a Christian and loving God, let's discuss some other expectations that are non-negotiable.

Employment

First and foremost, he should have a job. If it is the man's responsibility to take care of his family, how in the world is that possible if he does not have a job? Let's take it a step further. He should not even approach you for a date unless he is gainfully employed. Being employed is not just about having a job or having money, it represents his desire and willingness to provide for himself and take care of his personal responsibilities. If he cannot take care of himself, how is he going take care of you if he is unemployed? This is another potential red flag; you need to find out why he can't keep a job. Is this a situational issue (e.g., company layoff, company downsizing, or company out of business) or a habitual issue (e.g., he cannot keep a job). You also need to know how he is paying his bills if he is not working. Follow the money trail, it just may lead back to his parents or another woman.

Ladies, it is an insult and a red flag for a man to think he does not have to work. I am not talking about men who cannot work due to physical disabilities. I am talking about men who choose not to work. Second Thessalonians 3:10 warns, "[I]f any should not work neither should he eat!" Translation: If a man does not work, he does not eat! In case you are wondering, he also should not be coming to your house to eat either. As a single woman, you should not be inviting a man to your house for dinner, and you should not be accepting invitations to his house. (First Thessalonians 5:22 tells of avoiding the very appearance of evil.) That is why they have restaurants. Do not set yourself up for lustful temptations. However, you can avoid the situation altogether by explaining to him up front that all dates will be in a public venue or with other Christian couples.

If you believe it is okay to start dating him while he is unemployed, he will believe it is acceptable to be unemployed when you are engaged and after you are married. Once his unemployed status grows old, and it will, and you confront the issue (not him), then he will ask, "If it was okay in the beginning, why is it a problem now?" Do not start habits and behaviors if you do not plan on allowing them to continue.

Jailhouse Romances

The media tends to argue that there are more women than men, and in some cities and countries that may be true. However, if you are trusting God to choose your husband for you, those statistics do not apply to you. What God has for you, it is for you. Therefore, you do not have to go to the jail or prison to find him. Remember the principle in Proverbs 22:18, which says, "[W]hosoever findeth a wife findeth a good thing and obtaineth favor of the Lord." Therefore, I'm sure God didn't put a jail/prison relationship together, because it violates scripture. I'm not saying that if someone has been in jail, you shouldn't marry them. What I am saying is God didn't put the two of you together while he was in jail.

Let's look at this from another perspective. If he gets incarcerated while you are dating, you need to seek God and obey His instructions about continuing on in the relationship. While in jail or prison, he does not have the physical, emotional, and spiritual means to support you in any way. He has nothing to offer you but will expect you to provide for his physical, emotional, and spiritual needs. How? You will spend your gas to visit him. Depending on how far the place is, that could be a day's journey back and forth. You will use the money that God blessed you with for your family's needs to put on his books. He will call you collect using your minutes and asking you to put more money on his books and to come visit him. Do not let your fear of being alone cause you to continue in a relationship that drains your resources from the very beginning. You also have to remember that unless he allows God to renew his mind and transform his thinking, the chances of being incarcerated again are greater. Seek God and intercede for this man; that may be all God wants you to do from this point forward.

Ministry Worker, Not Pew Warmer

If you read the first part of this chapter, then you already know that "the head of every man is Christ; and the head of the woman is the man, and the head of Christ is God" (1 Corinthians 11:3). If you want your boyfriend or fiancé to be the head of your life and your family, then you need to know how he is serving God in his life. Being a pew warmer is for new Christians, not someone who claims to be ready to accept the role of spiritual leader for his entire family.

Whether he is singing in the choir, driving the church van, or cleaning God's house, he should be doing something that shows his willingness to serve God. If he is serving God when he is single, there is a greater chance that he will do so once he is married. This is key because you must know that your prospective husband has a heart and mind to serve God and God's people, which includes his wife and children. God's kingdom is vast, so even if he is not working in his home church, he should be working in some part of the God's kingdom.

Bridled Conversations

Despite reality television's depiction that it is impossible to have a conversation without curse words, it is possible and normal for many people. Therefore, you should expect him to bridle his tongue whether he is in mixed company or not. Colossians 4:6 instructs, "[L]et your speech be always with grace, season with salt, that you may know how ye should answer every man." He should expect the same from you also. Men and women alike use profanity in every conversation because that is how they choose to talk. You should have the ability and self-control to verbally express yourself without using profanity. "Let no corrupt communication proceed out of your mouth, but that which is good to the use of edifying, that it may minister grace unto the hearers" (Ephesians 4:29).

As a representative of God, your conversations must build one up, not tear them down. "Death and life [are] in the power of the tongue: and they that love it shall eat the fruit thereof" (Proverbs 18:21). You will learn to control your words when you learn to control your thoughts. "Let the words of my mouth, and the meditation of my heart, be acceptable in thy sight, O Lord, my strength, and my redeemer" (Psalms 19:14.) With what you think and what you speak, allow God to change how you think, and you will be able to change how you speak.

Chivalry Lives On

Unfortunately, too many women think chivalry is dead. There should be an expectation that your fiancé or boyfriend is a gentleman at all times, meaning you should be treated with respect all the time. He should open the door for you, pull the chair from the table, and compliment you on your attire, just to name a few. We, as women, have become so independent that we make men believe that we do not need them. Allowing a man to do these things for you is not a sign of weakness. It is actually an indication of your inner strength as a woman. It takes a strong, humble, godly woman to let the man in her life take the lead. Men need to know that they are needed, that you trust him to lead you. If you lead too long, you just may find yourself leading by yourself.

Affirming One Another

Do you enjoy hearing the words "I love you," "Great Job!" "I'm proud of you?" If you do, don't you think he does too? What is wrong with being kind? What is wrong with being nice? What is wrong with being loving, considerate, thoughtful, and understanding, not because you want a proposal, but because it is the right thing to do? A requirement for providing affirmation and support is placing someone else's needs before yours. It is not about having your way all the time, so if you are known for being a spoiled brat, this is going to be a serious challenge for you. Being supportive requires patience, endurance, kindness, and most of all, selfless love. You must have the other person's best interest at heart, without expecting anything in return, including an engagement ring.

A man's self-esteem needs building just like ours, if not more. Parents teach their sons to fight. Life teaches women how to fight just for survival and preservation. The battle scars we receive make us rough and tough. We can trample on a man's heart (ego) just with our attitude and never speak a word. However, we must allow God to transform us into gentle women. We must work toward having this meek and quiet spirit, which is of great price in the sight of God according to 1 Peter 3:4. I like to call this growing phase the gentle side of me.

We must know how to gently approach the man in our life with gentle words, gentle hands, gentle attitudes, and gentle thoughts. It is true that men are physically stronger than us, but have you ever had to deal with a wounded man? You must handle him with kit gloves for a man has a very delicate heart. Be gentle, but do not baby him. That is insulting and will leave him feeling emasculated, which should not be your intention. Remember he is not only that special man in your life but he is your Brother in Christ.

Help him to always present his best self. If you know your boyfriend or fiancé is fashionably challenged, please do not let him think the shirt is gray when it is not. By the same token, do not make him feel incompetent because he could not tell the difference. With gentleness, say something like, "Sweetie, you might want to look at that shirt in the light. I can see how you'd think that it is gray because it is so close to the color in your tie, but it's not. What about wearing this shirt instead?" Whatever you suggest, make sure it is better than what he was going to wear. Now he may not like your help the first time you correct him. However, once his friends and family start complimenting him on his new fashion style, he will be grinning from ear to ear. As you build him up as a man, he will strive to become the man God created him to be and a husband He created him to be for you.

Peace and Happiness

Relationships are challenging no matter how much you love one another, and there will be plenty of times when you will get on each other's nerves before and after the wedding. However, even in the midst of the most chaotic times, there should always be a feeling of peace within your spirit about the man to whom you are engaged or dating. If you are going to be in a relationship, don't you think you should enhance one another's life, instead of entangling it with grief and strife? If you do not treat them with the respect, love, and gentleness of Christ, someone else will.

There is an old saying, "I can do bad all by myself! I don't need any help being miserable!" What do you think, ladies! Is that quote true? Of course, it is! You can be financially, emotionally, physically, and spiritually miserable by yourself. You do not need another adult bringing their baggage to help you be even more miserable. Therefore, have an expectation of happiness in your relationships. Expect to have respect, love, honesty, loyalty, and trust as its core elements. These are all qualities that you, as a woman, should have in your own life. How can you expect these things from a man if you don't possess them within yourself?

Bringing It Full Circle

Ladies, these are realistic expectations that should be nonnegotiable. Your expectations should build him up, not tear him down, and his expectations of you should do the same. They protect you as a woman and keep you rooted and grounded in the realities of your relationship as God reveals them to you.

Act the age of the relationship. If you have been dating for six months, then act like it is a six-month-old relationship. Do not start acting like you have been dating for six years. I know men move fast, but so do we with our false expectations. Having healthy, respectful, and realistic expectations is a must when dating (even with your friendships). Just remember that you are not his mother and not his wife, just like he is not your father or husband. When you focus on truth (that you are not each other's parent or spouse) and operate from that perspective, you will stay on track with God's plan for your life. It is when you allow your mind to take you faster and further than the relationship is destined to go that you oftentimes get into trouble.

Do not get distracted by someone else's relationship. That has destroyed many potential relationships because we think we want what someone else has because we think it is better than what we have right now. Give yourself time to observe, experience, and enjoy each other in all seasons of the relationship and the emotions within those seasons: anger, sadness, happiness, excitement, joy, mourning, and stress.

Look for the red flags we discussed in chapter 10 and know that it is okay to move forward or move on. Be willing to listen to those who love you. They may see things in him that you cannot see because you are too close to the situation or too distracted by your emotions. All of our hope and expectations of being taken care of should be in the LORD JESUS CHRIST. *He is our true husband* according to Isaiah 54:5, "For thy maker [is] thine husband; the LORD of hosts [is] his name; and thy Redeemer the Holy One of Israel; the God of the whole earth shall he be called."

Woman to Woman

My dear sisters, my desire in writing this book is not to dampen your desire to be married but to make you think about marriage as God does, so you will not settle for any Joe Blow that comes your way with a ring and a smile. You must consider what is right and best for you according to the Word of God. Oftentimes, we accept anyone who comes along because we do not want to be alone. We look at our circumstances, age, weight, children, or barrenness and decide that we have to settle because something is better than nothing. God is here to tell you that you do not and should not settle for anything less than His very best for you. He just needs you to listen and trust Him. If you are willing to trust someone who does not owe you anything, why not trust the One who "gave his everything (His Son Jesus Christ), that whosoever believeth in him should not perish, but have everlasting life?" (John 3:16).

Being Honest with God

1. _____?

2. _____?

3. _____?

4. _____?

Journaling with God

13

FIREPROOF YOUR RELATIONSHIP (EPHESIANS 6:10–17)

> Finally, my brethren, be strong in the Lord, and in the power of his might. Put on the whole armour of God, that ye may be able to stand against the wiles of the devil

BEFORE YOU SPEND too much time thinking this chapter is about protecting your relationship with the man in your life, let me assure you that this chapter is not about him. "If it's not about him, then what relationship do I have to fireproof?" you may be asking. Well, after reading the first twelve chapters, what relationship should be the number one relationship in your life? After reading twelve chapters, I hope you said your relationship with Jesus!

Ephesians 6:12 states that "we wrestle not against flesh and blood, but against principalities, against powers, against the rulers of the darkness of this world, against spiritual wickedness in high places." As Christians, we know that the more we live for God, the more Satan attacks our faith in God. Therefore, before you can learn to protect your natural relationship with the man you love, you must first learn how to protect your spiritual relationship with the Father who loves you.

Since Satan attacks anything that honors God, you must learn to fireproof your relationship using weapons representing God. Second Corinthians 10:3–5 reminds us,

> For we walk in the flesh, we do not war after the flesh: (For the weapons of our warfare are not carnal, but mighty through God to the pulling down of strongholds;) casting down imaginations and every high thing that exalteth itself against the knowledge of God, and bringing into captivity every thought to the obedience of Christ.

To learn what those weapons are, go to Ephesians 6:13–17 and complete the following prebattle plan:

13. Take unto you the whole _____ of God.

14. Stand therefore, having your loins girt about with _____, and having on the breastplate of _____;
15. And your feet shod with the _____ of the gospel of _____.
16. Above all, taking the shield of _____.
17. And take the helmet of _____ and sword of the Spirit, which is the _____ of _____.

Please understand that fireproofing your relationship with God is not just a one-time event. It is something that must be done daily through prayer, meditation, and studying God's Word. It will require fasting and consecration (e.g., time alone with God). Fasting may not be from food, it may be from television, secular music, certain friends, or even the man in your life. Periods of fasting and consecration will be whatever God wants it to be. Will you obey His plan in order to fireproof your relationship with Him? Remember, if you have trouble submitting to God as a single woman, you will have double trouble submitting to your husband when you are married.

Fight for your relationship with God by staying in your word and in prayer. I know this Christian life is not an easy one to live, but I also know that we are not alone. God is fighting with us as well as protecting us from unseen danger. He will protect you, guide you, and keep you. Play with Satan, and he (Satan) will watch you die an eternal death; you will never know the fullness of what God has for you. The choice is yours.

Woman to Woman

We do not know what the future holds—only God does. For this reason, remember the serenity prayer:

> God, grant me the serenity to accept the things I cannot change; courage to change the things I can; and wisdom to know the difference. Living one day at a time; Enjoying one moment at a time; Accepting hardships as the pathway to peace; Taking, as He did, this sinful world as it is, not as I would have it; Trusting that He will make all things right if I surrender to His Will; That I may be reasonably happy in this life and supremely happy with Him Forever in the next. Amen.

Read Proverbs 8 (the entire chapter). This is real fireproofing at work: having God's wisdom to make right decisions based on God's truth. Fireproof your relationship with God first so you will be better able to fireproof your relationship with your future husband, even during the dating and engagement stages.

Being Honest with God

1. _____?

2. _____?

3. _____?

4. _____?

Journaling with God

14

DREAM BIG!

But as it is written, Eye hath not seen, nor ear heard, neither have entered into the heart of man, the things which God hath prepared for them that love him.

—1 Corinthians 2:9

Dream big! This book's content has been based on the possibility of getting married, but we've also talked the possibility that this is not the season for marriage for you. Do you not still dream big? Of course not. Why, you may ask? Because you have a big God.

If your season is being a mother, then dream big for yourself. Meaning, be the best mom this world has ever seen on this side of heaven, and then begin to dream big for your children. Children don't dream big until those big dreams have been prayed and placed in their hearts and minds. Martin Luther King said, "I have a dream," and the world is still talking about that dream.

Yes, dream big. In whatever state you find yourself, dream big. Dream big for your family, because it is on the wings of your dreams and prayers that they will become a reality in your life and your children's lives. The child that was told he or she would never amount to anything many times found himself in jail or in bondage to some sinful habit, all because someone sowed a seed of doubt and became a dream smasher instead of a dream builder.

Dreams are nothing more than goals God has placed in your heart. The Bible said in Proverbs 29:17–18: "Correct thy son, and he shall give thee rest; yea, he shall give delight unto thy soul. Where [there is] no vision, the people perish: but he that keepeth the law, happy [is] he."

This correction should be our thinking as well as our children's thinking, which then gives them a vision of hope a dream that will carry them through the future with expectation of God delivering a life and plan that they themselves could only imagine.

Another scripture that was personally given to me is in the book of Habakkuk 2:2–3: "And the Lord answered me, and said, Write the vision, and make [it] plain upon tables, that he may run that readeth it. For the vision [is] yet for an appointed time, but at the end it shall speak, and not lie: though it tarry, wait for it; because it will surely come, it will not tarry."

I praise God for his words of wisdom. This verse is clear—dream big; it might not happen today but it will happen. Whatever God whispers into your spirit, remember it and obey the scripture and write it down, and most of all believe and wait on it because God's promises always come true.

Come on, ladies, let's dream big no matter what you're praying for and waiting on God to fulfill in your life. Dream big because we serve a big God!

Being Honest with God

1. _____?

2. _____?

3. _____?

4. _____?

Journaling with God

15

Now That You Know

Believe me when I say that it has been a journey to try and tell you everything that I believe God wants you to know about being a godly woman in waiting. I know that the desire to be married is real, but your desire to live your life according to God's Word and His plan must be more important than being a wife (help meet).

As Christian women, we owe it to the lost world to be different, to be that light in a darkened world. Most importantly, we owe it to God. Unfortunately, we are blending in more and more to the point that you cannot tell the difference between Christians and non-Christians. We forget the scripture that says we are a peculiar people (see 1 Peter 2:9). Let the truth be told, most of us do not even know it exists. This scripture goes on to say that God called us out of the darkness into His marvelous light.

God created us so that everything we do should bring people to Him. Waiting and desiring to be married should do the same thing. While Hollywood and many people in this world—Christians as well as those who are not Christians—would have you believe it is okay to have sex outside of marriage, live together to figure it out, and play church, it is not okay, and God is not pleased. We are not to take our advice and cues from the world but from God. Acts 5:29 instructs, "We ought to obey God rather than man."

Now you know God is waiting on you to take your instructions from Him—not the world, not your pastor, not your best friend, not your parents, and not even me. Even with my best intentions, I can get it wrong too. Seek God and get His opinion first. Then everything else will fall into place.

The well-known scripture in Proverbs 3:5–6 says, "Trust in the Lord with all thine heart; and lean not unto thine own understanding. In all thine ways acknowledge Him [act like you know him] and he will direct thy path."

Afterword

My dear sisters, my sincere prayer for you is if you truly want to be a help meet (i.e., wife) one day, God will answer you with a resounding "Yes!" When He does, he will also bring you the man He chose just for you.

I pray that you will be patient in waiting on God as he prepares you and your husband to meet. You never know what day that will be, so be ready physically, mentally, financially, and spiritually. Be God's best as a woman so He will give you His best husband specifically created for you.

I hope this book has blessed your life and changed your thinking about God's expectations of you as a godly woman in waiting. If you do not know Him as your personal Lord and Savior, I pray that you will ask Him into your heart today. It is easy as ABC.

A—Admit that you are a sinner. Romans 3:23 says, "For all have sinned and come short of the glory of God."

B—Believe in your heart. Romans 10:10 concludes, "For with the heart man believeth unto righteousness; and with the mouth confession is made unto Salvation."

C—Confess with your mouth to Him (Jesus). Romans 10:9 promises, "That if thou shalt confess with thy mouth the Lord Jesus, and shalt believe in thine heart that God hath raised him from the dead, thou shalt be saved."

"For God so loved the world, that he gave his only begotten son, that whosoever believeth in him should not perish, but have everlasting life. God sent not his son into the world to condemn the world; but that the world through him might be saved" (John 3:16–17).

I want to give you something of value, and the only thing I can give you that is of any value is the Word of God. With that being said, I want to share with you my life verse:

"Let your light so shine before men, that they may see your good works, and glorify your Father which is in heaven" (Matthew 5:16).

I sincerely hope you have enjoyed the book, which I believe is part of my good works. May God continue to richly bless you!

About the Author

Rosiland Brown, simply known to family and friends as Roz or Rozzie, is a mother, grandmother, minister, teacher, author, and inspirational speaker. She loves her family, her friends, and most of all the Lord Jesus Christ. As a single mother of two and the spiritual mother of many, she knows firsthand the joys and challenges of walking with God. As a woman who desires to live a life completely surrendered and sold out to Christ, she also understands the joys and challenges of being single and desiring to be married. Having helped God on two prior occasions and marrying outside of His will, she learned the painful consequences of living life outside of God's will especially in the area of marriage. It is from her life's experiences and through God's grace and mercy that she passes these pearls of wisdom on to you.

www.ingramcontent.com/pod-product-compliance
Lightning Source LLC
Chambersburg PA
CBHW030320080526
44584CB00012B/640